Edward James Corbett CIE VD (25 July 1875 – 19 April 1955) was a British hunter, tracker, naturalist, and author who hunted a number of man-eating tigers and leopards in India. He held the rank of colonel in the British Indian Army and was frequently called upon by the Government of the United Provinces of Agra and Oudh, now the Indian states of Uttar Pradesh and Uttarakhand, to kill man-eating tigers and leopards that were preying on people in the nearby villages of the Kumaon-Garhwal Regions.

He authored **Man-Eaters of Kumaon**, Jungle Lore, and other books recounting his hunts and experiences, which enjoyed critical acclaim and commercial success. He became an avid photographer and spoke out for the need to protect India's wildlife from extermination.

CONTENTS

JIM CORBETT

THE MAN-EATING LEOPARD OF RUDRAPRAYAG

SANAGE PUBLISHING HOUSE

Paperback: 978-939089619-6

Sanage Publishing House LLP
Mumbai, India

sanagepublishing@gmail.com

THE PILGRIM ROAD

If you are a Hindu from the sun-scorched plains of India and you desire—as all good Hindus do—to perform the pilgrimage to the age- old shrines of Kedarnath and Badrinath, you must start on your pilgrimage from Hardwar and, in order to acquire a full measure of the merits vouch¬safed to you for the correct performance of the pilgrimage, you must walk every step of the way from Hardwar to Kedarnath and, thence, over the mountain track to Badrinath, barefoot.

Having purified yourself by immersion in the sacred Har-ki-pauri pool, done *darshan* at the many shrines and temples in Hardwar, and added your mite to their coffers, you must not omit to toss a coin within reach of the festering stumps—which once were hands—of the lepers who line the narrowest part of the pilgrim road above the sacred pool, for if you make this omission, they will call down curses on your head. What matter if these unfortunate ones have wealth beyond your dreams secreted in their filthy rags, or in the rock caves they call their homes? The curses of such as they were best avoided, and immunity will cost you but a few coppers.

You have now done all that custom and religion require of a good Hindu and are at liberty to start on your long and hard pilgrimage.

The first place of interest you will come to after leaving Hardwar is Rishikesh. Here you will make your first acquaintance with the Kalakamli Wallahas, so called because of the black blanket their founder wore—and which many of his disciples still wear—-in the form of a habit or loose cloak bound round the middle with a cord of goat's hair; and who are renowned throughout the land for their good deeds. I do not know if any of the other religious brotherhoods you will meet on your pilgrimage have any claim to renown, but I do know that the Kalakamli Wallahas have such a claim, and justly so, for out of the offerings they receive at their many shrines and temples, they have built—and they maintain— hospitals, dispensaries, and pilgrim shelters, and they feed the poor and the needy.

With Rishikesh behind you, you will come next to Lachman *Jhula*, where the pilgrim road crosses from the right to the left bank of the Ganges on a suspension bridge. Here beware of the red monkeys who infest the bridge, for they are even more importunate than the lepers of HardWar, and if you omit to propitiate them with offerings of sweets, or parched gram, your passage across the long and narrow bridge is likely to be both difficult and painful.

Three-day's journey up the left bank of the Ganges and you have reached the ancient capital of Garhwal—Shreenagar—an historic, religious, and trading centre of considerable importance and of great beauty, nestling in a wide, open valley surrounded by high mountains. It was here, in the year 1805, that the forebears of the Garhwali soldiers who have fought so gallantly in two world wars made their last, and unsuccessful, stand against the Gurkha invaders, and it is a matter of great regret to the people of Garhwal that their ancient city of Shreenagar, together with the palaces of their kings, was swept away, to the last stone, by the bursting of the Gohna Lake dam in 1894. This dam, caused by a landslide in the valley of the Birehi Ganga, a tributary of the Ganges, was 11,000 feet wide at the base, 2,000 feet wide at the summit, and 900 feet high and, when it burst, ten billion cubic feet of water were released in the short space of six hours. So well was the bursting of the dam timed that though the flood devastated the valley of the Ganges right down to Hardwar and swept away every bridge, only one family was lost, the members of which had returned to the danger-zone after having been forcibly removed from it.

From Shreenagar you have to face a stiff climb to Chatikhal, which is compensated for by the magnificent views you will get of the Ganges valley and of the eternal snows above Kedarnath.

A day's march from Chatikhal and you see in front of you Golabrai with its row of grass-thatched pilgrim shelters, a one-roomed stone-built house, and its drinking trough. This big and imposing drinking trough is fed by a tiny crystal-clear stream which, in summer, is sedately conducted down the mountain-side by a series of channels rough-hewn from pine saplings. At other seasons of the year the water cascades unconfined and merrily over rocks draped with moss and maidenhair fern, through luxuriant beds of vivid green watercress and sky-blue strobilanthes.

A hundred yards beyond the pilgrim shelters, and on the right-hand side of the road, stands a mango tree. This tree and the two-storied house above it which is the home of the *pundit*, who owns the Golabrai pilgrim shelters, are worthy of note, for they play an important part in the tale I have to tell.

Another two miles, along the last flat bit of ground you will see for many a day, and you have reached Rudraprayag, where you and I, my pilgrim friend, must part, for your way lies across the Alaknanda and up the left bank of the Mandakini to Kedarnath, while mine lies over the mountains to my home in Naini Tal.

The road in front of you, which has been trodden by the feet of millions of pilgrims like you, is excessively steep and incredibly rough; and you, whose lungs have never breathed air above sea level, who have never climbed anything higher than the roof of your house, and whose feet have never trodden anything harder than yielding sand, will suffer greatly. Times there will be, a-many, when, gasping for breath, you toil ..up the face of steep mountains on feet torn and bleeding by passage over rough rocks, sharp shale, and frozen ground, when you will question whether the prospective reward you seek is worth the present price you pay in suffering; but being a good Hindu you will toil on, comforting yourself with the thought that merit is not gained without suffering, and the greater the suffering in this world, the greater the reward in the next.

THE MAN-EATER

Prayag' is the Hindi word for 'confluence'. At Rudraprayag, two rivers—the Mandakini coming down from Kedarnath, and the Alaknanda from Badrinath—meet, and from here onwards the combined waters of the two rivers are known to all Hindus as Ganga Mai, and to the rest of the world as the Ganges.

When an animal, be it a leopard or be it a tiger, becomes a man-eater, it is given a place-name for purposes of identification. The name so given to a man-eater does not necessarily imply that the animal began its man- eating career at, or that all its kills were confined to, that particular place. It is quite natural that the leopard which started its man-eating career at a small village twelve miles from Rudraprayag, on the Kedarnath pilgrim route, should have been known for the rest of its career as the Man-eating Leopard of Rudraprayag.

Leopards do not become man-eaters for the same reasons that tigers do. Though I hate to admit it, our leopards—the most beautiful and the most graceful of all the animals in our jungles, and who when cornered or wounded are second to none in courage—are scavengers to the extent that they will, when driven by hunger, eat any dead thing they find in the jungle, just as lions will in the African bush.

The people of Garhwal are Hindus, and as such cremate their dead. The cremation invariably takes place on the bank of a stream or river in order that the ashes may be washed down into the Ganges and eventually into the sea. As most of the villages are situated high up on the hills, while the streams of rivers are in many cases miles away down in the valleys, it will be realized that a funeral entails a considerable tax on the man-power of a small community when, in addition to the carrying party, labour has to be provided to collect and carry the fuel needed for the cremation. In normal times these rites are carried out very effectively; but when disease in epidemic form sweeps through the hills, and the inhabitants, the faster than they can be disposed of, a very simple rite, which consists of placing a live coal in the mouth of the deceased, is performed in the village, and the body is then carried to the edge of the hill and cast into the valley below.

A leopard, in an area in which his natural food is scarce, Ending these bodies, very soon acquires a taste for human flesh, and when the disease dies down and normal conditions are re-established, he, very naturally, .'on finding his food-supply cut off, takes to killing human beings. In the wave of epidemic influenza that swept through the country in 1918 and that cost India over a million lives, Garhwal suffered very severely, and it was at the end of this epidemic that the Garhwal man-eater made his appearance.

The first human kill credited to the man-eating leopard of Rudraprayag is recorded as having taken place at Bainji village on 9 June 1918, and the last kill for which the man-eater was responsible took place at Bhainswara village on 14 April 1926. Between these two dates the number of human kills recorded by Government was one hundred and twenty-five.

While I do not think that this figure, of one hundred and twenty-five, is out to the extent claimed by Government officials who served in Garhwal at that time and by residents in the area in which the man-eater was operating, I do know that the figure given is not correct, for some kills which took place while I was on the ground have not been shown in the records.

In crediting the man-eater with fewer kills than he was actually responsible for, I do not wish to minimize in any way the sufferings endured by the people of Garhwal for eight long years, nor do I wish to detract in any way from the reputation of the animal which the people of Garhwal claim as having been the most famous man-eating leopard of all time.

However, be the number of human kills what they may, Garhwal can claim that this leopard was the most publicized animal that has ever lived, for he was mentioned—to my knowledge—in the press of the United Kingdom, America, Canada, South Africa, Kenya, Malaya, Hong Kong, Australia, New Zealand, and in most of the dailies and weeklies in India.

In addition to this newspaper publicity, tales of the man-eater were carried to every part of India by the sixty thousand pilgrims who annually visit the shrines of Kedarnath and Badrinath.

The procedure laid down by Government in all cases of human beings alleged to have been killed by man-eaters is for the relatives or friends of the deceased to lodge a report with the village *patwari* as soon after the occurrence as possible. On receipt of the report the *patwari* proceeds to the spot, and if the body of the victim has not been found before his arrival he organizes a search party, and with their aid endeavours to find the victim. If the body has been found before his arrival, or if the search party finds it, the *patwari* holds an inquiry on the spot and when satisfied that it is a genuine kill by a man-eater, and not a case of murder, he gives the relatives permission to remove the remains for cremation or for burial, according to the caste or creed of the victim. The kill is duly recorded in his register against the man-eater operating in that area, and a full report of occurrence is submitted to the administrative head of the district—the Deputy Commissioner—who also keeps a register in which all the man- eater's kills are recorded. In the event, however, of the body, or any portion of it, not being found—as sometimes happens, for man-eaters have an annoying habit of carrying their victims for long distances—the case is held over for further inquiry, and the man-eater is not credited with the kill. Again, when people are mauled by a man-eater and subsequently die from their injuries, the man-eater concerned is not credited with their deaths.

It will thus be seen that though the system adopted for recording the kills of man-eaters is as good as it can be, it is possible for one of these abnormal animals to be responsible for more human kills than he is finally credited with, especially when his operations extend over a long period of years.

TERROR

The word 'terror' is so generally and universally used in connection with everyday trivial matters that it is apt to fail to convey, when intended to do so, its real meaning. I should like therefore to give you some idea of what terror—real terror—meant to the fifty thousand inhabitants living in the five hundred square miles of Garhwal in which the man-eater was operating, and to the sixty thousand pilgrims who annually passed through that area between the years 1918 and 1926. And I will give you a few instances to show you what grounds the inhabitants, and the pilgrims, had for that terror.

No curfew order has ever been more strictly enforced, and more implicitly obeyed, than the curfew imposed by the man-eating leopard of Rudraprayag.

During the hours of sunlight life in that area carried on in a normal way. Men went long distances to the bazaars to transact business, or to outlying villages to visit relatives or friends; women went up the mountain-sides to cut grass for thatching or for cattle-fodder; children went to school or into the jungles to graze goats or to collect dry sticks, and, if it was summer, pilgrims, either singly or in large numbers, toiled along the pilgrim routes on their way to and from the sacred shrines of Kedarnath and Badrinath.

As the sun approached the western horizon and the shadows lengthened, the behaviour of the entire population of the area underwent a very sudden and a very noticeable change. Men who had sauntered to the bazaars or to outlying villages were hurrying home; women carrying great bundles of grass were stumbling down the steep mountain-sides; children who had loitered on their way from school, or who were late in bringing in their flocks of goats or the dry sticks they had been sent out to collect, were being called by anxious mothers, and the weary pilgrims were being urged by any local inhabitant who passed them to hurry to shelter.

When night came, an ominous silence brooded over the whole area— no movement and no sound anywhere. The entire local population was behind fast-closed doors and, in many cases, had sought further protection by building additional doors. Those of the pilgrims who had not been fortunate enough to find accommodation inside houses were huddled close together in pilgrim shelters. And all, whether in house or shelter, .Were silent for fear of attracting the dread man-eater.

This is what terror meant to the people of Garhwal, and to the pilgrims, for eight long years.

I will now give a few instances to show you what grounds there were for that terror.

() () ()

A boy, an orphan aged fourteen, was employed to look after a flock of forty goats. He was of the depressed—untouchable—class, and each evening when he returned with his charges he was given his food and then shut into a small room with the goats. The room was on the ground floor of a long row of double-storied buildings and was immediately below the room occupied by the boy's master, the owner of the goats. To prevent the goats crowding in on him as he slept, the boy had fenced off the far left- hand corner of the room.

This room had no windows and only one door, and when the boy and the goats were safely inside, the boy's master pulled the door to, and fastened it by passing the hasp, which was attached by a short length of chain to the door, over the staple fixed in the lintel. A piece of wood was then inserted in the staple to keep the hasp in place, and on his side of the door the boy, for his better safety, rolled a stone against it.

On the night the orphan was gathered to his fathers, his master asserts the door was fastened as usual, and I have no reason to question the truth of his assertion. In support of it, the door showed many deep claw-marks, and it is possible that in his attempts to claw open the door the leopard displaced the piece of wood that was keeping the hasp in place, after which it would have been easy for him to push the stone aside and enter the room.

Forty goats packed into a small room, one corner of which was fenced off; could not have left the intruder much space to manoeuvre in, and it is left to conjecture whether the leopard covered the distance from the door to the boy's corner of the room over the backs of the goats or under their bellies, for at this stage of the proceedings all the goats must have been on their feet.

It were best to assume that the boy slept through all the noise the leopard must have made when trying to force open the door, and that the goats must have made when the leopard had entered the room, and that he did not cry for help to deaf ears, only screened from him and the danger that menaced him by a thin plank.

After killing the boy in the fenced-off corner, the leopard carried him across the empty room—the goats had escaped into the night—down a steep hillside, and then over some terraced fields to a deep boulder-strewn ravine. It was here, after the sun had been up a few hours, that the master found all that the leopard had left of his servant.

Incredible as it may seem, not one of the forty goats had received so much as a scratch.

() () ()

A neighbour had dropped in to spend the period of a long smoke with a friend. The room was L-shaped and the only door in it was not visible from where the two men sat on the floor with their backs to the wall, smoking. The door was shut but not fastened, for up to that night there had been no human kills in the village. The room was in darkness and the owner of it had just passed the hookah to his friend when it fell to the ground, scattering a shower of burning charcoal and tobacco. Telling his friend to be more careful or he would set the blanket on which they were sitting on fire, the man bent forward to gather up the embers and, as he did so, the door came into view. A young moon was near setting and, silhouetted against it, the man saw a leopard carrying his friend through the door.

When recounting the incident to me a few days later the man said: T am speaking the truth, *sahib*, when I tell you 1 never heard even so much as the intake of a breath, or any other sound, from my friend who was sitting only an arm's-length from me, either when the leopard was killing him, or when it was carrying him away. There was nothing I could do for my friend, so I waited until the leopard had been gone some little while, and then I crept up to the door and hastily shut and secured it.'

The wife of the Headman of a village was ill from a fever, and two friends had been called in to nurse her.

() () ()

There were two rooms in the house. The outer room had two doors, one opening on to a small flagged courtyard, and the other leading into the inner room. This outer room also had a narrow slip of a window set some four feet above floor level, and in this window, which was open, stood a large brass vessel containing drinking water for the sick woman.

Except for the one door giving access to the outer room, the inner room had no other opening in any of its four walls.

The door leading out on to the courtyard was shut and securely fastened, and the door between the two rooms was wide open.

The three women in the inner room were lying on the ground, the sick woman in the middle with a friend on either side of her. The husband in the outer room was on a bed on the side of the room nearest the window, and on the floor beside his bed, where its light would shine into the inner ro6m, was a lantern, turned down low to conserve oil.

Round about midnight, when the occupants of both the rooms were asleep, the leopard entered by way of the narrow slip of a window, avoiding in some miraculous way knocking over the brass vessel which nearly filled it, skirted round the man's low bed and, entering the inner room, killed the sick woman. It was only when the heavy brass vessel crashed to the floor as the leopard attempted to lift its victim through the window that the sleepers awoke.

When the lantern had been turned up the woman who had been

sick was discovered lying huddled up under the window, and in her throat were four great teeth-marks.

A neighbour, whose wife had been one of the nurses on that night, when relating the occurrence to me said, 'The woman was very ill from her fever and was likely to have died in any case, so it was fortunate that the leopard selected her.'

() () ()

Two Gujars were moving their herd of thirty buffaloes from one grazing- ground to another, and accompanying them was the twelve-year-old daughter of the older of the two men, who were brothers.

They were strangers to the locality and either had not heard of the man-eater or, which is more probable, thought the buffaloes would give them all the protection they needed.

Near the road and at an elevation of eight thousand feet was a narrow strip of flat ground below which was a sickle-shaped terraced field, some quarter of an acre in extent, which had long been out of cultivation. The men selected this site for their camp and having cut stakes from the jungle which surrounded them on all sides, they drove them deep into the field and tethered their buffaloes in a long row.

After the evening meal prepared by the girl had been eaten, the party of three laid their blankets on the narrow strip of ground between the road and the buffaloes and went to sleep.

It was a dark night, and some time towards the early hours of the morning the men were awakened by the booming of their buffalo-bells and by the snorting of the frightened animals. Knowing from long experience that these sounds indicated the presence of carnivora, the men lit a lantern and went among the buffaloes to quieten them, and to see that none had broken the ropes tethering them to the stakes.

The men were absent only a few minutes. When they returned to their sleeping-place they found that the girl whom they had left asleep was missing. On the blanket on which she had been lying were big splashes of blood.

When daylight came the father and the uncle followed the blood trail. After skirting round the row of tethered buffaloes, it went across the narrow field and down the steep hillside for a few yards, to where the leopard had eaten his kill.

'My brother was born under an unlucky star, *sahib*, for he has no son, and he had only this one daughter who was to have been married shortly, and to whom he looked in the fullness of time to provide him with an heir, and now the leopard has come and eaten her.'

() () ()

I could go on and on, for there were many kills, and each one has its own tragic story, but I think I have said enough to convince you that the people of Garhwal had ample reason to be terrified of the man-eating leopard of Rudraprayag, especially when it is remembered that Garhwalis are intensely superstitious and that, added to their fear of physical contact with the leopard, was their even greater fear of the supernatural, of which I shall give you an example.

I set out from the small one-roomed Rudraprayag Inspection Bungalow one morning just as day was breaking, and as I stepped off the verandah I saw in the dust, where the ground had been worn away by human feet, the pugmarks of the man-eater.

The pugmarks were perfectly fresh and showed that the leopard had stepped out of the verandah only a few minutes in advance of me, and from the direction in which they were pointing it was evident that the leopard, after his fruitless visit to the bungalow, was making for the pilgrim road some fifty yards away.

Tracking between the bungalow and the road was not possible owing to the hard surface of the ground, hut as I reached the gate I saw the pugmarks were heading in the direction of Golabrai. A large flock of sheep and goats had gone down the road the previous evening, and in the dust they had kicked up the leopard's tracks showed up as clearly as they would have on fresh-fallen snow.

I had, by then, become quite familiar with the man-eater's pugmarks and could with little difficulty have distinguished them from the pugmarks of any hundred leopards.

A lot can be learnt from the pugmarks of carnivora, as for instance the sex, age, and size of the animal. I had examined the pugmarks of the man- eater yery carefully the first time I had seen them, and I knew he was an out-sized male leopard, long past his prime.

As I followed the tracks of the man-eater on this morning I could see that he was only a few minutes ahead of me, and that he was moving at a slow, even pace.

The road, which had no traffic on it at this early hour of the morning, wound in and out of a number of small ravines, and as it was possible that the leopard might on this occasion break his rule of never being out after daylight, I crept round each corner with the utmost care until I found, a mile farther on, where the leopard had left the road and gone up a great track into dense scrub and tree jungle.

A hundred yards from where the leopard left the road there was a small field, in the centre of which was a thorn enclosure, erected by the owner of the field to encourage packmen to camp there and fertilize it. In this enclosure was the flock of sheep and goats that had come down the road the previous evening.

The owner of the flock, a rugged fellow who by the looks of him had been packing trade commodities up and down the pilgrim road for nigh on half a century, was just removing the thornbush closing the entrance to the enclosure when I came up. In reply to my inquiries he informed me that he had seen nothing of the leopard but that, just as dawn was breaking, his two sheep-dogs had given tongue and, a few minutes later, a *kakar* had barked in the jungle above the road.

When I asked the old packman if he would sell me one of his goats, he asked for what purpose it was wanted; and when 1 told him it was to tie up for the man-eater, he walked through the opening in the fence, replaced the bush, accepted one of my cigarettes, and sat down on a rock by the side of the road.

We remained smoking for a while, with my question still unanswered, and then the man began to talk.

'You, *sahib*, are undoubtedly he whom I have heard tell of on my way down from my village near Badrinath, and it grieves me that you should ' have come all this long way from your home on a fruitless errand. The evil spirit that is responsible for all the human deaths in this area is not an animal, as you think it is, that can be killed by ball or shot, or by any of the other means that you have tried and that others have tried before you; and in proof of what I say I will tell you a story while I smoke this second cigarette. The story was told to me by my father, who, as everyone knows, had-never been heard to tell a lie.

'My father was a young man then, and I unborn, when an evil spirit, like the one that is now troubling this land, made its appearance in our village, and all said it was a leopard. Men, women, and children were killed in their homes and every effort was made, as has been made here, to kill the animal. Traps were set, and far-famed marksmen sat in trees and fired ball and shot at the leopard; and when all these attempts to kill it had failed, a great terror seized the people and none dared leave the shelter of his home between the hours of sunset and sunrise.

'And then the headmen of my father's village, and of the villages round about, bade all the men attend a *panchayat*, and when all were assembled the *panch* addressed the meeting and said they were assembled to devise some fresh means to rid themselves of this man-eating leopard. Then an old man, fresh back from the burning-ghat, whose grandson had been killed the previous night, arose and said it was no leopard that had entered his house and killed his grandson as he lay asleep by his side, but one from among their own community who, when he craved for human flesh and blood, assumed the semblance of a leopard, and that such a one could not be killed by the methods already tried, as had been amply proved, and could only be killed by fire. His suspicions, he said, fell on the fat *sadhu* who lived in the hut near the ruined temple.

'At this there was a great uproar, some exclaiming that the old man's sorrow at the loss of his grandson had demented him; others averring he was right. And these later recalled that the *sadhu* had arrived at the village at about the time the killings had started, and it was further recalled that on the day succeeding a killing the *sadhu* had been wont to sleep all day, stretched on his bed in the sun.

'When order had been restored the matter was long debated and the *panchayat* eventually decided that no immediate action would be taken, but that the *sadhu*'s movements should in future be watched. The assembled men were then divided into three parties, the first party to start its watch from the night the next kill could be expected; for the kills had taken place at more or less regular intervals.

'During the nights the first and the second parties were on watch, the *sadhu* did not leave his hut.

'My father was with the third party, and at nightfall he silently took up his position. Soon after, the door of the hut slowly opened, and the *sadhu* emerged and vanished into the night. Some hours later an agonized scream came floating down on the night air from the direction of a charcoal- burner's hut far up the mountain-side, and thereafter there was silence.

'No man of my father's party closed an eye that night, and as the grey dawn was being born in the east they saw the *sadhu* hurrying home, and his hands and his mouth were dripping blood.

'When the *sadhu* had gone inside his hut and had closed the door, the watchers went up to it, and fastened it from the outside by passing the chain that was dangling from it over the staple in the lintel. Then they went each to his haystack and returned with a big bundle of straw, and when the sun rose that morning there was nothing but smouldering ash where the hut had been. From that day the killing stopped.

'Suspicion has not yet fallen on any one of the many *sadhus* in these parts, but when it does the method employed in my father's time will be adopted in mine, and until that day comes, the people of Garhwal must suffer.

'You have asked if I will sell you a goat. I will not sell you a goat, *sahib*, for I have none to spare. But if, after hearing my story, you still want an animal to tie up for what you think is a man-eating leopard, I will lend you one of my sheep. If it is killed you shall pay me its price, and if it is not killed no money shall pass between us. Today and tonight I rest here, and tomorrow at the rising of the Bhootia star I must be on my way.'

Near sundown that evening I returned to the thorn enclosure and my packman friend very cheerfully let me select from his flock a fat sheep which I considered was heavy enough to give the leopard two nights' feed. This sheep I tied in the scrub jungle close to the path up which the leopard had gone some twelve hours earlier.

Next morning I was up betimes. As I left the bungalow I again saw the pugmarks of the man-eater where he had stepped off the verandah, and at the gate I found he had come up the road from the direction of Golabrai, and, after calling at the bungalow, had gone away towards the Rudraprayag bazaar.

The fact that the leopard was trying to secure a human kill was proof that he had no interest in the sheep I had provided for him, and I was therefore not surprised to find that he had not eaten any portion of the •sheep which he had apparently killed shortly after I had tied it up.

'Go back to your home, *sahib*, and save your time and your money,' was the parting advice of the old packman as he whistled to his flock, and headed down the road for Hardwar.

A parallel case, happily without as tragic an ending, occurred a few years previously near Rudraprayag.

Incensed at the killing of their relatives and friends, and convinced that a human being was responsible for their deaths, an angry crowd of men seized an unfortunate *sadhu* of Kothgi village, Dasjulapatty, but before they were able to wreak their vengeance on him, Philip Mason, then Deputy Commissioner of Garhwal, who was camping in the vicinity, arrived on the scene. Seeing the temper of the crowd, and being a man of great experience, Mason said he had no doubt that the real culprit had been apprehended but that before the *sadhu* was lynched justice demanded that his guilt should be established. To this end he suggested that the *sadhu* should be placed under arrest and closely guarded, night and day. To this suggestion the crowd agreed, and for seven days and seven nights the *sadhu* was carefully guarded by the police, and as carefully watched by the populace. On the eighth morning, when the guard and the watchers were being changed, word was brought that a house in a village some miles away had been broken into the previous night, and a man carried off.

The populace raised no objection to the *sadhu* being released that day, contenting themselves by saying that on this occasion the wrong man had been apprehended, but that next time no mistake would be made.

In Garhwal all kills by man-eaters are attributed to *sadhus*, and in Naini Tal and Almora districts all such kills are attributed to the Bokhsars, who dwell in the unhealthy belt of grass at the foot of the hills called the Terai, living chiefly on game. The *sadhus* are believed to kill for the lust of human flesh and blood, and the Bokhsars are believed to kill for the jewellery their victims are wearing, or for other valuables they have on their person. More women than men have been killed by man-eaters in Naini Tal and Almora districts, but for this there is a better reason than the one given.

() () ()

I have lived too long in silent places to be imaginative. Even so there were times a-many during the months I spent at Rudraprayag sitting night after night—on one occasion for twenty-eight nights in succession—watching "bridges, or cross-roads, or approaches to villages, or over animal or human kills, when I could imagine the man-eater as being a big, light-coloured animal—for so he had appeared to me the first time that I saw him—with the body of a leopard and the head of a fiend.

A fiend who, while watching me through the long night hours, rocked and rolled with silent fiendish laughter at my vain attempts to outwit him, and licked his lips in anticipation of the time when, finding me off my guard for one brief moment, he would get the opportunity he was waiting for, of burying his teeth in my throat. It may be asked what the Government was doing all the years the Rudraprayag man-eater menaced the people of Garhwal. I hold no brief for the Government, but after having spent ten weeks on the ground, during which time I walked many hundreds of miles and visited most of the villages in the affected area, I assert that the Government did everything in its power to remove the menace. Rewards were offered: the local population believed they amounted to ten thousand rupees in cash and the gift of two villages, sufficient inducement to make each one of the four thousand licensed gun-holders of Garhwal a prospective slayer of the man-eater. Picked *shikari*s were employed on liberal wages and were promised special rewards if their efforts were successful. More than three hundred special gun licences over and above the four thousand in force were granted for the specific purpose of shooting the man-eater. Men of the Garhwal Regiments stationed in Lansdowne were permitted to take their rifles with them when going home on leave, or were provided with sporting arms by their officers. Appeals were made through the press to sportsmen all over India to assist in the destruction of the leopard. Scores of traps of the drop-door type, with goats as bait, were erected on approaches to villages and on roads frequented by the man-eater. *Patwari*s and other Government officials were supplied with poison for the purpose of poisoning human kills, and, last but not least, Government servants, often at great personal risk, spent all the time they could spare from their official duties in pursuit of the man-eater.

The total results from all these many and combined efforts were a slight gunshot wound which creased the pad of the leopard's left hind foot and shot away a small piece of skin from one of its toes, and an entry in Government records by the Deputy Commissioner of Garhwal that, so far from suffering any ill effects, the leopard appeared to thrive on, and be stimulated by, the poison he absorbed via human kills.

Three interesting incidents are recorded in a Government report and I will summarize them here.

First: In response to the press appeal to sportsmen, two young British officers arrived at Rudraprayag in 1921 with the avowed object of shooting the man-eater. What reason they had for thinking that the leopard crossed from bank to bank of the Alaknanda river by the Rudraprayag suspension bridge I do not know; anyway they decided to confine their efforts to this bridge and shoot the leopard as it was crossing at night. There are towers at each end of the bridge to carry the suspending cables, so one of the young sportsmen sat on the tower on the left bank of the river, and his companion sat on the tower on the right bank.

After they had been sitting for two months on these towers, the man on the left bank saw the leopard walk out on to the bridge from the archway below him. Waiting until the leopard had got well on to the bridge, he fired, and as it dashed across, the man on the tower on the right bank emptied the six chambers of his revolver at it. Next morning blood was found on the bridge and on the hill up which the leopard had gone, and as it was thought that the wound, or wounds, would be fatal, a search was kept up for many days. The report goes on to say that for six months after it was wounded the leopard did not kill any human beings.

I was told about this incident by men who had heard the seven shots, and who had assisted in trying to recover the wounded animal. It was thought by the two sportsmen, and also by my informants, that the leopard had been hit in the back by the first bullet and possibly in the head by some of the subsequent bullets, and it was for this reason that a diligent and prolonged search had been made for it. From the particulars given me of the blood trail I was of the opinion that the sportsmen were wrong in thinking that they had inflicted a body and head wound on the leopard, for the blood trail as described to me could only have been made by a foot wound, and I was very gratified to find later that my deductions were correct and that the bullet fired by the man on the tower on the left bank had only creased the pad of the leopard's left hind foot and shot away a portion of one of its toes, and that the man on the right bank had missed all his shots.

Second: After some twenty leopards had been caught and killed in traps of the drop-door type, a leopard which everyone thought was the man-eater was caught in one of these traps; and as the Flindu population were unwilling to kill it for fear the spirits of the people whom the man- eater had killed would torment them, an Indian Christian was sent for. This Christian was living in a village thirty miles away, and before he ,' could arrive on the scene, the leopard had dug its way out of the trap, and escaped.

Third: After killing a man the leopard lay up with his kill in a small isolated patch of jungle. Next morning, when search was being made for the victim, the leopard was detected leaving the jungle. After a short chase it was seen to enter a cave, the mouth of which was promptly closed with thornbushes heaped over with big rocks. Every day a growing crowd of men visited the spot. On the fifth day, when some five hundred were assembled, a man whose name is not given but whom the report described as 'a man of influence' came, and, to quote the report, 'said scornfully "there is no leopard in this cave" and took the thorns off the cave. As he took the thorns up, the leopard suddenly rushed out of the cave and made his way safely through a crowd of some five hundred persons who had gathered there.'

These incidents took place shortly after the leopard had become a man-eater, and had the leopard been killed on the bridge, shot in the trap, or sealed up in the cave, several hundred people need not have died, and Garhwal would have been saved many years of suffering.

ARRIVAL

It was during one of the intervals of Gilbert and Sullivan's *Yeomen of the Guard*, which was showing at the Chalet Theatre in Naini Tal in 1925, that I first had any definite news of the Rudraprayag man-eater.

I had heard casually that there was a man-eating leopard in Garhwal and had read articles in the press about the animal, but knowing that there were over four thousand licensed gun-holders in Garhwal, and a host of keen sportsmen in Lansdowne, only some seventy miles from Rudraprayag, I imagined that people were falling over each other in their eagerness to shoot the leopard and that a stranger under these circumstances would not be welcome.

It was with no little surprise therefore that, as I stood at the Chalet bar that night having a drink with a friend, I heard Michael Keene— then Chief Secretary to the Government of the United Provinces and later Governor of Assam—telling a group of men about the man-eater and trying to persuade them to go after it. His appeal, judging from the remark of one of the group, and endorsed by the others, was not received with any enthusiasm. The remark was, 'Go after a man-eater that has killed a hundred people? Not on your life!'

Next morning I paid Michael Keene a visit and got all the particulars I wanted. He was not able to tell me exactly where the man-eater was operating, and suggested my going to Rudraprayag and getting in touch with Ibbotson. On my return home I found a letter from Ibbotson on my table.

Ibbotson—now Sir William Ibbotson, and lately Adviser to the Governor of the United Provinces—had very recently been posted to Garhwal as Deputy Commissioner, and one of his first acts had been to try to rid his district of the man-eater. It was in this connection that he had written to me.

My preparations were soon made, and by travelling via Ranikhet, Adbadri, and Karanprayag, I arrived on the evening of the tenth day at a Road Inspection Bungalow near Nagrasu. When leaving Naini Tal I did not know it was necessary to arm myself with a permit to occupy this bungalow, and as the caretaker had orders not to allow anyone to occupy it unless so armed, the six Garhwalis carrying my kit, my servant, and I toiled on for another two miles down the Rudraprayag road until we found a suitable place on which to camp for the night.

While my men busied themselves getting water and dry sticks, and my servant collected stones for a cooking-place, I picked up an axe and went to cut down thornbushes to make an enclosure to protect us during the night, for we had been warned ten miles farther up the road that we had entered the man-eater's territory.

Shortly after the fires to cook our evening meal had been lit, a very agitated call came down to us from a village far up the mountain-side, asking us what we were doing out in the open, and warning us that if we remained where we were one or more of us would surely be killed by the man-eater. When the good Samaritan had delivered his warning, to do which he had possibly taken a great risk—for it was then dark—Madho Singh, whom you have met elsewhere,[1] expressed the wishes of all present when he said, 'We will stay here, *sahib*, for there is sufficient oil in the lantern to keep it alight all night, and you have your rifle.'

There was sufficient oil in the lantern to keep it alight all night, for I found it burning when I awoke in the morning, and my loaded rifle lay across my bed. But the thorn enclosure was very flimsy and we were dead tired after our ten days' march, and if the leopard had paid us a visit that night he would have secured a very easy victim.

Next day we arrived at Rudraprayag and were given a warm welcome by the men whom Ibbotson had instructed to meet us.

---

1 'See 'The Chowgarh Tigers' in *Man-eaters ofKumaon*.

INVESTIGATION

I shall not attempt to give you a day-by-day account of my activities during the ten weeks I spent at Rudraprayag, for it would be difficult after this lapse of time to write such an account and, if written, it would be boring for you to read. I shall confine myself to relating a few of my experiences, sometimes while alone and at other times in company with Ibbotson. But before doing so I should like to give you some idea of the country over which the leopard ranged for eight years, and in which I hunted him for ten weeks.

If you were to climb the hill to the east of Rudraprayag you would be able to see the greater portion of the five hundred square miles of country that the Rudraprayag man-eater ranged over. This area is divided into two more or less equal parts by the Alaknanda river, which, after passing Karanprayag, flows south to Rudraprayag, where it is met by the Mandakini coming down from the northwest. The triangular bit of country between the two rivers is less steep than the country along the left bank of the Alaknanda, and there are consequently more villages in the former area than in the latter.

From your elevated position, the cultivated land in the distance shows up as a series of lines drawn across the face of the steep mountains. These lines are terraced fields which vary in width from a yard to, in some cases, fifty or more yards. The village buildings, you will note, are invariably set at the upper end of the cultivated land; this is done with the object of overlooking and protecting the cultivation from stray cattle and wild animals, for except in very rare cases there are no hedges or fences round the fields. The brown and the green patches that make up most of the landscape are, respectively, grassland and forests. Some of the villages, you will observe, are entirely surrounded by grasslands, while others are entirely surrounded by forests. The whole country, as you look down on it, is rugged and rough, and is cut up by innumerable deep ravines and rock cliffs. In this area there are only two roads, one starting from Rudraprayag and going up to Kedarnath, and the other the main pilgrim road to Badrinath. Both roads, up to the time I am writing about, were narrow and rough and had never had a wheel of any kind on them.

The number of human beings killed between 1918 and 1926 is shown below.

THE MAN-EATING LEOPARD OF RUDRAPRAYAG CASUALTY LIST

(by villages), 1918-1926

Six kills

CHOPRA

Five kills

KOTHKI, RATAURA

Four kills

BIJRAKOT

Three kills

NAKOT, GANDHARI, KOKHANDI, DADOLI, QUETHI, JHIRMOLI GOLABRAI, LAMERI

Two kills

BAJADU, RAMPUR, MAIKOTI, CHHATOLI, KOTI, MADOLA, RAUTA, KANDE (JOGI), BAWRUN, SARI, RANAU, PUNAR, TILANI, BAUNTHA, NAGRASU, GWAR, MARWARA

One kill

ASON, PILU, BHAUNSAL, MANGU, BAINJI, BHATWARI, KHAMOLI, SWANRI, PHALSI, KANDA DHARKOT, DANGI, GUNAUN, BHATGAON, BAWAL, BARSIL, BHAINSGAON, NARI, SANDAR, TAMEND, KHATYANA, SEOPURI, SAN, SYUND, KAMERA, DARMARI, DHAMKA BELA, BELA-KUND,

SAUR, BHAINSARI, BAJNU, QUILI, DHARKOT, BHAINGAON, CHHINKA, DHUNG, KIURI, BAMAN KANDAI, POKHTA, THAPALGAON, BANSU, NAG, BAISANI, RUDRAPRAYAG, GWAR, KALNA, BHUNKA, KAMERA, SAIL, PABO, BHAINSWARA

ANNUAL TOTALS

1918	...	1
1919	...	3
1920	...	6
1921	...	23
1922	...	24
1923	...	26
1924	...	20
1923	....	8
1926	...	14
		125

It would be reasonable to assume that more human beings would have been killed in villages surrounded by forests than in villages surrounded by cultivated land. Had the man-eater been a tiger this would undoubtedly have been the case, but to a man-eating leopard, which only operates at night, the presence or absence of cover makes no difference, and the only reason why there were more kills in one village than in another was due, in the one case, to lack of precautions, and in the other, to the observance of them.

I have mentioned that the man-eater was an out-sized male leopard long past his prime, but though he was old he was enormously strong. The ability of carnivora to carry their kills to a place where they can feed undisturbed determines, to a great extent, the place they choose to do their killing. To the Rudraprayag man-eater all places were alike, for he was capable of carrying the heaviest of his human victims for distances up to—on one occasion that I know of—four miles. On the occasion I refer to the leopard killed a fully grown man in his own house and carried his victim for two miles up the steep slope of a well-wooded hill, and down the far side for another two miles through dense scrub jungle. This was done for no apparent reason, for the kill had taken place in the early hours of the night and the leopard had not been followed up until noon of the next day.

() () ()

Leopards—other than man-eaters—are the most easily killed of all animals in our jungles, for they have no sense of smell.

More methods are employed in killing leopards than are employed in killing any other animal. These methods vary according to whether the leopard is being killed for sport, or for profit. The most exciting, and the most interesting, method of killing leopards for sport is to track them down in the jungles and, when they are located, stalk and shoot them. The easiest, and the most cruel, method of killing leopards for profit is to insert a small and very highly explosive bomb in the flesh of an animal which are been killed by a leopard. Many villagers have learnt to make these bombs, and when one of them comes in contact with the leopard's teeth, it explodes and blows the leopard's jaws off. Death is instantaneous in some cases, but more often than not the unfortunate animal crawls away to die a lingering and very painful death, for the people who use the bombs have not the courage to follow the blood trail left by the leopard to dispatch it.

() () ()

The tracking, locating, and stalking of leopards, besides being exciting and interesting, is comparatively easy. For leopards have tender pads and keep to footpaths and game tracks as far as possible; they are not hard to locate, for practically every bird and animal in the jungle assists the hunter; and they are easy to stalk, for, though they are blessed with very keen sight and hearing, they are handicapped by having no sense of smell. The sportsman can therefore select the line of approach that best suits him, irrespective of the direction in which the wind is blowing.

Having tracked, located, and stalked a leopard, far more pleasure is got from pressing the button of a camera than is ever got from pressing the trigger of a rifle. In the one case the leopard can be watched for hours, and there is no more graceful and interesting animal in the jungles to watch. The button of the camera can be pressed as fancy dictates to make a record which never loses its interest. In the other case a fleeting glimpse, one press of the trigger, and—if the aim has been true—the acquisition of a trophy which soon loses both its beauty and its interest.

THE FIRST KILL

Shortly before my arrival at Rudraprayag, Ibbotson had organized a beat which if it had been successful would have saved the lives of fifteen human beings. The beat, and the circumstances leading up to it, are worthy of record.

Twenty pilgrims toiling up the road to Badrinath arrived towards evening at a small roadside shop. After the shopkeeper had met their wants he urged them to be on their way, telling them there was only just sufficient daylight left for them to reach the pilgrim shelters four miles farther up the road, where they would get food and safe shelter. The pilgrims were unwilling to accept this advice; they said they had done a long march that day and were too tired to walk another four miles, and that all they wanted were facilities to prepare and cook their evening meal, and permission to sleep on the platform adjoining the shop. To this proposal the shopkeeper vigorously objected. He told the pilgrims that his house was frequently visited by the man-eater, and that to sleep out in the open would be to court death.

While the argument was at its height a *sadhu* on his way from Mathura to Badrinath arrived on the scene and championed the cause of the pilgrims. He said that if the shopkeeper would give shelter to the women of the party he would sleep on the platform with the men, and if any leopard—man-eater or otherwise—dared to molest them he would take it by the mouth and tear it in half.

To this proposal the shopkeeper had perforce to agree. So while the ten women of the party took shelter in the one-roomed shop behind a locked door, the ten men lay down in a row on the platform, with the *sadhu* in the middle.

When the pilgrims on the platform awoke in the morning they

found the *sadhu* missing, the blanket on which he had slept rumpled, and the sheet he had used to cover himself with partly dragged off the platform and spotted with blood. At the sound of the men's excited chattering the shopkeeper opened the door, and at a glance saw what had happened. When the sun had risen, the shopkeeper, accompanied by the men,

followed the blood trail down the hill and across three terraced fields, to a low boundary wall; here, lying across the wall, with the lower portion of his body eaten away, they found the *sadhu*.

Ibbotson was staying at Rudraprayag at this time, trying to get in touch with the man-eater. There had been no kills during his stay, so he decided to beat, on spec, a very likely looking bit of cover, on the far side of the Alaknanda, which the locals suspected was used by the man-eater as a lying-up place during the hours of daylight. So while the twenty pilgrims were toiling up the road towards the little shop, the *patwari*s and other members of Ibbotson's stalf were going round the near-by villages warning men to be ready for the beat which was to take place on the morrow.

After an early breakfast next morning Ibbotson accompanied by his wife and a friend whose name I have forgotten, and followed by some members of his staff and two hundred beaters, crossed the Alaknanda by the suspension bridge, went up the hill on the far side for a mile or so, and took up positions for the beat.

While the beat was still in progress, word was brought by runner of the killing of the *sadhu*.

The beat, which proved to be a blank, was completed and a hurried council held, the upshot of which was that Ibbotson, his party, and the two hundred beaters set off up the right bank, to cross the river four miles farther up by a swing bridge, to make their way back along the left bank to the scene of the kill, while the staff dispersed over the countryside to collect as many men as possible and assemble them at the shop.

By late afternoon two thousand beaters and several additional guns had gathered, and the high rugged hill above the shop was beaten from top to bottom. If you know Ibbotson, there is no need for me to tell you that the beat was very efficiently organized, and as efficiently carried out, and the only reason why it failed in its object was that the leopard was not in that area.

When a leopard, or a tiger, leaves of his own accord a kill in the open, in an exposed spot, it is an indication that the animal has no further interest in the kill. After its feed it invariably removes itself to a distance, maybe only two or three miles, or in the case or man-eaters, maybe to a distance of ten or more miles. So it is quite possible that, while the hill was being beaten, the man-eater was peacefully slumbering ten miles away.

LOCATING THE LEOPARD

Man-eating leopards are of rare occurrence, and for this reason very little is known about them.

My own experience of these animals was very limited, amounting to no more than a brief encounter with one many years previously, and though I suspected that the change-over from animal to human-and- animal diet would affect the habits of a leopard as much as it does those of a tiger, I did not know to what extent a leopard's habits would change, and meanwhile I decided to try to kill the man-eater by the methods usually employed for killing leopards.

The most common method of killing leopards is to sit up for them, either over a kill or over live bait in the form of a goat or a sheep. To carry out either one of these methods it is necessary in the one case to find a kill, and in the other to locate the quarry.

My object in going to Rudraprayag was to try to prevent further loss of human life, and I had no intention of waiting for another human kill to occur over which I could sit, therefore the obvious thing to do was to locate the man-eater and shoot it over live bait.

Here a formidable difficulty, which I hoped in time partly to overcome, presented itself. From the maps I had been supplied with I found that the man-eater was operating over an area of roughly five hundred square miles. Five hundred square miles of country anywhere would have been a considerable area in which to find and shoot any animal, and in this mountainous and rugged part of Garhwal the task of finding an animal that only operated at night appeared, at first glance, to be well-nigh impossible—until I took the Alaknanda river, which divided the area into two more or less equal parts, into consideration.

It was generally believed that the Alaknanda offered no obstacle to the man-eater and that when he found it difficult to obtain a human kill on one bank, he crossed over to the other bank, by swimming the river.

I discounted this belief. No leopard in my opinion would under any circumstances voluntarily commit itself to the swift-flowing, ice-cold waters of the Alaknanda, and I was convinced that when the man-eater crossed from one bank to the other he did so by one of the suspension bridges.

There were two suspension bridges in the area, one at Rudraprayag, and the other about twelve miles farther up the river, at Chatwapipal. Bfetween these two bridges there was a swing bridge—the one by which Ibbotson, his party, and the two hundred men had crossed the river on the day of the beat. This swing bridge, which no animal excepting a rat could possibly have crossed, was the most fear-compelling structure of its kind that I have ever seen. The two hand-twisted grass cables, blackened by age and mouldy from the mists rising from the river, spanned some two hundred feet of foaming white water which, a hundred yards farther down, surged with a roar like thunder between two walls of rock, where a *kakar*, driven by wild dogs, is credited with having leapt across the Alaknanda. Between the cables, and forming the footway, were odd bits of sticks an inch and a half to two inches in diameter set about two feet apart and loosely tied to the cables with wisps of grass. To add to the difficulty in crossing this cobweb structure, one of the cables had sagged, with the result that the sticks on which one had to place one's feet were at an angle of forty-five degrees. The first time I met this fearsome *jhula* I was foolish enough to ask the toll-collector, who for the payment of one pice permitted me to risk my life on it, whether the bridge was ever tested or repaired. His answer, given as he ran a speculative eye over me, that the bridge was never tested or repaired but was replaced when it broke under the weight of someone who was trying to cross it, gave me a cold feeling down my spine, a feeling that remained with me long after I had got safely to the other side.

This *jhula* being beyond the powers of the man-eater to cross, there remained the two suspension bridges, and I felt sure that if I could close them against the leopard I should be able to confine him to one side of the Alaknanda, and so reduce by half the area in which to look for him.

The first thing therefore was to try to find out on which bank of the river the leopard was. The last kill, of the *sadhu*, had taken place on the left bank of the river a few miles from the Chatwapipal suspension bridge, and I felt sure that the leopard had crossed this bridge, after abandoning his kill, for no matter what precautions the locals and the pilgrims may have taken before a kill, their precautions were redoubled immediately after one, and made it almost impossible for the leopard to secure consecutive kills in the same area. Looking at the map you will ask why, if this was so, as many as six kills have been shown against a single village. I can only answer that an effort cannot be sustained indefinitely. The houses are small and without conveniences or means of sanitation, and it would not be surprising if, hearing the man-eater was operating in a village ten, fifteen, or.rwenty miles away, some man, woman, or child should, at the urgent dictate of nature, open a door for a brief minute and so give the leopard the chance for which he had perhaps been waiting many nights.

THE SECOND KILL

No photographs or other means by which I could identify the man-eater by his pugmarks were available, so, until I had been given an opportunity of acquiring this information for myself, I decided to treat all leopards in the vicinity of Rudraprayag as suspect, and to shoot any that gave me a chance.

The day I arrived at Rudraprayag, I purchased two goats. One of these I tied up the following evening a mile along the pilgrim road; the other I took across the Alaknanda and tied up on a path running through some heavy scrub jungle where I found the old pugmarks of a big male leopard. On visiting the goats the following morning I found the one across the river had been killed and a small portion of it eaten. The goat had unquestionably been killed by a leopard, but had been eaten by a small animal, possibly a pine-marten.

Having received no news about the man-eater during the day, I decided to sit up over the goat, and at 3 p.m. took up my position in the branches of a small tree about fifty yards from the kill. During the three hours I sat in the tree I had no indication, from either animals or birds, that the leopard was anywhere in the vicinity, and as dusk was falling I slipped off the tree, cut the cord tethering the goat—which the leopard had made no attempt to break the previous night—and set off for the bungalow.

I have already admitted that I had very little previous experience of man-eating leopards, but I had met a few man-eating tigers, and from the time I left the tree until I reached the bungalow I took every precaution to guard against a sudden attack; and it was fortunate that I did so.

I made an early start next morning, and near the gate of the bungalow I picked up the tracks of a big male leopard. These tracks

I followed back to a densely wooded ravine which crossed the path close to where the goat was lying. The goat had not been touched during the night.

The leopard that had followed me could only have been the man-eater, and for the rest of the day I walked as many miles as my legs would carry me, telling all the people in the villages I visited, and all whom I met on the roads, that the man-eater was on our side of the river, and warning them to be careful.

Nothing happened that day, but next day, just as I was finishing breakfast after a long morning spent in prospecting the jungles beyond Golabrai, a very agitated man dashed into the bungalow to tell me that a woman had been killed by the man-eater the previous night in a village on the hill above the bungalow—the same hill and almost at the exact spot from where you obtained your bird's-eye view of the five hundred square miles of country the man-eater was operating over.

Within a few minutes I collected all the things I needed—a spare rifle and a shotgun, cartridges, rope, and a length of fishing-line—and set off up the steep hill accompanied by the villager and two of my men. It was a sultry day, and though the distance was not great—three miles at the most—the climb of four thousand feet in the hot sun was very trying and I arrived at the village in a bath of sweat.

The story of the husband of the woman who had been killed was soon told. After their evening meal, which had been eaten by the light of the fire, the woman collected the metal pots and pans that had been used and carried them to the door to wash, while the man sat down to have a smoke. On reaching the door the woman sat down on the doorstep, and as she did so the utensils clattered to the ground. There was not sufficient light for the man to see what had happened, and when he received no answer to his urgent call he dashed forward and shut and barred the door. 'Of what use,' he said, 'would it have been for me to risk my life in trying to recover a dead body?' His logic was sound, though heartless; and I gathered that the grief he showed was occasioned not so much by the loss of his wife, as by the loss of that son and heir whom he had expected to see born within the next few days.

The door, where the woman had been seized, opened on to a four- foot-wide lane that ran for fifty yards between two rows of houses. On hearing the clatter of the falling pots and pans, followed by the urgent call of the man to his wife, every door in the lane had been instantaneously shut. The marks on the ground showed that the leopard had dragged the unfortunate woman the length of the lane, then killed her, and carried her down the hill for a hundred yards into a small ravine that bordered some terraced fields. Here he ate his meal, and here he left the pitiful remains.

The body lay in the ravine at one end of a narrow terraced field, at the other end of which, forty yards away, was a leafless and stunted walnut tree in whose branches a hayrick had been built, four feet from the ground and six feet tall. In this hayrick I decided to sit.

Starting from near the body, a narrow path ran down into the ravine. On this path were the pugmarks of the leopard that had killed the woman, and they were identical with the pugmarks of the leopard that had followed me two nights previously from the killed goat to the Rudraprayag bungalow. The pugmarks were of an out-sized male leopard long past his prime, with a slight defect where a bullet fired four years previously had creased the pad of his left hind paw.

I procured two stout eight-foot bamboos from the village and drove them into the ground close to the perpendicular bank that divided the field where the body was laying from the field below. To these bamboos I fixed my spare rifle and securely, tied lengths of dressed line to the triggers, looped the lines back over the trigger-guards, and fastened them to two stakes driven into the hillside on the far side of, and a little above, the path. If the leopard came along the path he had used the previous night there was a reasonable chance of his pulling on the lines and shooting himself; on the other hand, if he avoided them, or came by any other way, and I fired at him while he was on the kill, he would be almost certain to run into the trap which lay on his most natural line of retreat. Both the leopard, because of its protective colouring, and the body, which had been stripped of all clothing, would be invisible in the dark; so to give me an idea of the direction in which to fire, I took a slab of white rock from the ravine and put it on the edge of the field, about a foot from the near side of the body.

My ground arrangements completed to my satisfaction, I made myself a comfortable seat on the rick, throwing out some of the straw, and heaping some behind me and up to my waist in front. As I was facing the kill and had my back to the tree, there was little chance of the leopard seeing me, no matter at what time he came; and that he would come during the night, in spite of his reputation of not returning to his kills, I was firmly convinced. My clothes were still wet after the stiff climb, but a comparatively dry jacket kept out the chill wind; so I settled down into my soft and comfortable seat and prepared for an all-night vigil. I sent my men away, and told them to remain in the Headman's house until I came for them, or until the sun was well up next morning. (I had stepped from the bank on to the rick and there was nothing to prevent the man-eater from doing the same.)

The sun was near setting, and the view of the Ganges valley, with the snowy Himalayas in the background showing bluish-pink under the level rays of the setting sun, was a feast for the eyes. Almost before I realized it, daylight had faded out of the sky and night had come.

Darkness, when used in connection with night, is a relative term and has no fixed standard; what to one man would be pitch dark, to another ' would be dark, and to a third moderately dark. To me, having spent so much of my life in the open, the night is never dark, unless the sky is overcast with heavy clouds. I do not wish to imply that I can see as well by night as by day; but I can see quite well enough to find my way through any jungle or, for that matter, over any ground. I had placed the white stone near the body only as a precaution, for I hoped that the starlight, with the added reflection from the snowy range, would give me sufficient light to shoot by.

But my luck was out; for night had hardly fallen when there was a flash of lightning, followed by distant thunder, and in a few minutes the sky was heavily overcast. Just as the first big drops of a deluge began to fall, I heard a stone roll into the ravine, and a minute later the loose straw on the ground below me was being scratched up. The leopard had arrived; and while I sat in torrential rain with the icy-cold wind whistling through my wet clothes, he lay dry and snug in the straw below. The storm was one of the worst I have ever experienced, and while it was at its height, I saw a lantern being carried towards the village, and marvelled at the courage of the man who carried it. It was not until some hours later that I learnt that the man who so gallantly braved both the leopard and the storm had done a forced march of over thirty miles from Pauri to bring me the electric night-shooting light the Government had promised me; the arrival of this light three short hours earlier *might*. But regrets are vain, and who can say that the fourteen people who died later would have had a longer span of life if the leopard had not buried his teeth in their throats? And again, even if the light had arrived in time there is no certainty that I should have killed the leopard that night.

The rain was soon over—leaving me chilled to the bone—and the clouds were breaking up when the white stone was suddenly obscured, and a little later I heard the leopard eating. The night before, he had lain in the ravine and eaten from that side; so, expecting him to do the same this night, I had placed the stone on the near side of the kill. Obviously, the rain had formed little pools in the ravine, and to avoid them the leopard had taken up a new position and in doing so had obscured my mark. This was something I had not foreseen; however, knowing the habits of leopards, I knew I should not have to wait long before the stone showed up again. Ten minutes later the stone was visible, and almost immediately thereafter

I heard a sound below me and saw the leopard as a light-yellowish object disappearing under the rick. His light colour could be accounted for by old age, but the sound he made when walking I could not then, nor can I now, account for; it was like the soft rustle of a woman's silk dress, and could not be explained by stubble in the field—for there was none—or by the loose straw lying about.

Waiting a suitable length of time, I raised the rifle and covered the stone, intending to fire the moment it was again obscured; but there is a limit to the time a heavy rifle can be held to the shoulder, and when the limit had been reached I lowered the rifle to ease my aching muscles. I had hardly done so when the stone for the second time disappeared from view. Three times within the next two hours the same thing happened, and in desperation, as I heard the leopard approaching the rick for the fourth time, I leant over and fired at the indistinct object below me.

The narrow terrace to which I have given the usual name of 'field' was only about two feet wide at this point, and when I examined the ground next morning I found my bullet-hole in the centre of the two-foot-wide space with a little hair, cut from the leopard's neck, scattered round it.

I saw no more of the leopard that night, and at sunrise I collected my men and set off down the steep hill to Rudraprayag, whilst the husband and his friends carried away the woman's remains for cremation.

PREPARATIONS

My thoughts as, cold and stiff, I walked down the hill to Rudraprayag from the scene of my night's failure were very bitter, for, from whatever angle it was viewed, there was no question that the fickle jade chance had played both Garhwal and myself a scurvy trick which we did not deserve.

However little I merit it, the people of our hills credit me with supernatural powers where man-eaters are concerned. News that I was on my way to try to rid Garhwal of the man-eater had preceded me, and while I was still many days' march from Rudraprayag the men I met on the roads, and those who from their fields or village homes saw me passing, greeted me with a faith in the accomplishment of my mission that was as touching as it was embarrassing, and which increased in intensity the nearer I approached my destination. Had any been there to witness my entry into Rudraprayag, he would have found it hard to believe that the man whom the populace thronged round was no hero returning from the wars, but a man, very sensible of his limitations, who greatly feared that the task he had undertaken was beyond his powers of accomplishment.

Five hundred square miles, much of which was clothed with dense scrub jungle, and all of which was rugged and mountainous, was an enormous area in which to find and shoot one particular leopard out of possibly fifty that inhabited it, and the more I saw of the grand and beautiful country the less I liked it from the viewpoint of the task I had undertaken. The populace quite naturally did not share my misgivings; to them I was one who had rid others of man-eaters and who had now come among them to rid them of the menace they had lived under for eight long years. And then, with incredible good luck, I had within a few hours of my arrival got the animal I was in pursuit of to kill one of my goats and, by staying out a little after dark, to follow me to that side of the Alaknanda where I believed it would be less difficult to deal with it than it would have been on the other side. Following on this initial success had been the kill of the unfortunate woman. I had tried to prevent the further loss of human life, and had failed, and my failure had presented me with an opportunity of shooting the leopard which otherwise I might not have got for many months. As I had been toiling uphill behind my guide the previous day, I had weighed up my chances of killing the leopard and assessed them at two-tcf-one, despite the facts that the animal had in recent years earned the reputation of never returning to a kill, that it was a dark night, and that I had no aid to night shooting. The day I visited Michael Keene and told him I would go to Garhwal he had asked me if I had everything I wanted; and hearing that I only lacked a night-shooting light and would telegraph to Calcutta for one, he said the least the Government could do for me was to provide me with a light; and he promised to have the best one procurable waiting for me at Rudraprayag.

Though my disappointment was great when I found that the light had not arrived, it was mitigated by my ability to see in the dark, the ability on which I had assessed my chances at two-to-one. So much depended on the success of that night's venture, that I had armed myself with a spare rifle and shotgun, and when from my concealed position on the hayrick I viewed the scene—the short range at which I should get my shot, and the perfectly camouflaged gun-trap into which the leopard would of a certainty run if I missed or wounded him—my hopes rose high and I put my chances of success at ten-to-one. Then had come the storm. With visibility reduced to practically nil, and without the electric light, I had failed, and my failure would in a few hours be known throughout the stricken area.

Exercise, warm water, and food have a wonderfully soothing effect on bitter thoughts, and by the time I had picked my way down the steep hillside, had a hot bath, and breakfast, I had ceased to rail at fate and was able to take a more reasonable view of my night's failure. Regret over a bullet fired into the ground was as profitless as regret over milk spilt on sand, and provided the leopard had not crossed the Alaknanda my chances of killing it had improved, for I now had the electric shooting light which the runner had braved both the leopard and the storm to bring me.

The first thing to do was to find out if the leopard had crossed the Alaknanda, and as I was firm in my conviction that the only way it could do this was by way of the suspension bridges, I set out after breakfast to glean this information. I discounted the possibility of the leopard having crossed the Chatwapipal bridge, for no matter how great the shock he had received by the discharge of my heavy rifle a few feet from his head, it was not possible that he would have covered the fourteen miles that separated the kill from the bridge in the few hours that remained between the firing of my shot and daylight, so I decided to confine my search to the Rudraprayag bridge.

There were three approaches to the bridge; one from the north, one from the south, and between these two a well-beaten footpath from the Rudraprayag bazaar. After examining these approaches very carefully I crossed the bridge and examined the Kedarnath pilgrim road for half a mile, and then the footpath on which three nights previously my goat had been killed. Satisfied that the leopard had not crossed the river. I determined to put in operation my plan for closing the two bridges at night and thus confining the leopard to my side of the river, The plan was a simple one and, given the co-operation of the caretakers of the bridges, both of whom lived on the left bank and close to the bridge abutments, was certain of success.

To close the only means of communication between the two banks of the river over a stretch of some thirty miles would appear to be a very high-handed proceeding, but actually it was not so, for no human being dared to use the bridges between sunset and sunrise owing to the curfew imposed by the leopard.

The bridges were closed by wedging thornbushes in the four-foot- wide archway in the towers carrying the steel cables from which the plank footway was suspended, and during the whole period that the bridges were closed with thorn, or were guarded by me, no human being demanded passage across them.

I spent in all some twenty nights on the tower on the left bank of the Rudraprayag bridge, and those nights will never be forgotten. The tower was built out on a projecting rock and was twenty feet high, and the platform on the top of it, which had been worn smooth by the wind, was about four feet wide and eight feet long. There were two means of reaching this platform, one by swarming along the cables, which ran through holes near the top of the tower and were anchored in the hillside some fifty feet from the tower, and the other by climbing up a very rickety bamboo ladder. I chose the latter way, for the cables were coated over with some black and very evil-smelling matter which clung to one's hands and permanently stained one's clothes.

The ladder—two uneven lengths of bamboo connected with thin sticks loosely held in position with string—only reached to within four feet of the platform. Standing on the top rung of the ladder and dependent for a handhold on the friction of the palms of my hands on the smooth masonry, the safe gaining of the platform was an acrobatic feat that had less appeal the oftener it was tried.

All the rivers in this part of the Himalayas flow from north to south, and 'n the valleys through which they flow blows a wind which changes direction with the rising and the setting of the sun. During daylight hours the wind—locally called dadu—blows from the south, and during the hours of night it blows from the north.

At the time when I used to take up my position on the platform there was usually a lull in the wind, but shortly thereafter it started blowing as a light zephyr gaining in strength as daylight faded, and amounting by midnight to a raging gale. There was no handhold on the platform and even when lying flat on my stomach to increase friction and reduce wind-pressure, there was imminent risk of being blown off on to the rocks sixty feet below, off which one would have bounced into the ice-cold Alaknanda—not that the temperature of the water would have been of any interest after a fall of sixty feet on to sharp and jagged rocks. Strangely enough, whenever I felt in fear of falling it was always the water, and never the rocks, that I thought of. Added to the discomfort of the wind, I suffered torment from a multitude of small ants, which entered my clothes and ate away patches of skin. During the twenty nights I guarded bridge, the thornbushes were not placed in position; and in all that long period the bridge was only crossed by one living thing—a jackal.

MAGIC

Each evening when I went to the bridge I was accompanied by two men who carried the ladder that enabled me to climb to the platform, and which they removed after handing me my rifle.

On the second day, as we arrived at the bridge, we saw a man dressed in flowing white robes with something glinting on his head and breast. He carried a six-foot silver cross, and was approaching the bridge from the direction of Kedarnath. On reaching the bridge the man knelt down and, holding the cross in front of him, bowed his head. After remaining in this position for a little while he raised the cross high, rose to his feet, took a few steps forward, and again knelt down and bowed his head. This he continued to do at short intervals all the way across the long bridge.

As he passed me the man raised his hand in salutation, but since he appeared to be deep in prayer I did not speak to him. The glints I had seen on his head-dress and breast were, I perceived, silver crosses.

My men had been as interested in this strange apparition as I had been, and watching him climb the steep footpath to the Rudraprayag bazaar, they asked me what manner of man he was, and from what country he had come. That he was a Christian was apparent, and as I had not heard him speak I assumed from his long hair, jet-black luxuriant beard, and what I could see of his features, that he was a man from Northern India.

The following morning, when with the help of the ladder I had climbed down from the tower and was proceeding to the Inspection Bungalow, where I passed that portion of the daylight hours that I did not spend in visiting near and distant villages in search of news of the man-eater, I saw the tall white-robed figure standing on a great slab of rock near the road, surveying the river. At my approach he left the rock and greeted me, and when I asked him what had brought him to these parts he said he had come—from a distant land—to free the people of Garhwal from the evil spirit that was tormenting them. When I asked how he proposed accomplishing this feat, he said he would make an effigy of a tiger and after he had, by prayer, induced the evil spirit to enter it, he would set the effigy afloat on the Ganges and the river would convey it down to the sea from where it could not return, and where it would do no farther harm to human beings.

However much I doubted the man's ability to accomplish the task he.had set himself, I could not help admiring his faith and his industry. He arrived each morning before I left the tower, and I found him still at work when I returned in the evening, labouring with split bamboos, string, paper, and cheap coloured cloth on his 'tiger'. When the effigy was nearing completion a heavy rainstorm one night made the whole structure come unstuck, but, nothing daunted, he cheerfully started on it again next morning, singing as he worked.

Came at last the great day when the 'tiger'—about the size of a horse, and resembling no known animal—was fashioned to his satisfaction.

Who is there among our hill-folk who does not whole-heartedly enjoy taking part in a tamasha? When the effigy, tied to a long pole, was carried down a steep path to a small sandy beach, it had an escort of over a hundred men, many of whom were beating gongs and blowing long trumpets.

At the river's edge the effigy was unlashed from the pole. The white- robed man, with his silver crosses on headgear and breast and his six-foot cross in his hands, knelt on the sand, and with earnest prayer induced the evil spirit to enter his handiwork, and then the effigy, with a crash of gongs and blare of trumpets, was consigned to the Ganges, and speeded on its way to the sea by a liberal offering of sweets and flowers.

Next morning the familiar figure was absent from the rock, and when I asked some men who were on their way to have an early dip in the river where my friend of the flowing robes had come from, and where he had gone, they answered, 'Who can tell whence a holy man has come, and who dare question whither he has departed?'

These men with sandalwood-paste caste-marks on their foreheads, who spoke of the man as 'holy', and all those others who had taken part in the launching ceremony, were Hindus.

In India, where there are no passports or identity discs, and where religion counts for so much—except among those few who have crossed the 'black water'—I believe that a man wearing a saffron robe, or carrying a beggar's bowl, or with silver crosses on his headgear and chest, could walk from the Khyber Pass to Cape Comorin without once being questioned about his destination, or the object of his journey.

A NEAR ESCAPE

While I was still guarding the bridge, Ibbotson and his wife Jean arrived from Pauri, and as the accommodation in the Inspection Bungalow was very limited I moved out to make room for them, and set up my forty-pound tent on the hill on the far side of the pilgrim road.

A tent afforded little protection against an animal that had left his claw-marks on every door and window for miles round, so I helped my men to put a thorn fence round the ground we intended to camp on. Overhanging this plot of ground was a giant prickly-pear-tree, and as its branches interfered with the erection of the tent I told the men to cut it down. When the tree had been partly cut through I changed my mind, for I saw that I should be without shade during the heat of the day, so instead of felling the tree I told the men to lop the overhanging branches. This tree, which was leaning over the camp at an angle of forty-five degrees, was on the far side of the fence.

There were eight of us in the little camp, and when we had eaten our evening meal I wedged a thornbush securely into the opening in the fence we had entered by, and as I did so I noticed that it would be very easy for the man-eater to climb the tree and drop down on our side of the fence. However, it was too late then to do anything about it, and if the leopard left us alone for that one night, the tree could be cut down and removed in the morning.

I had no tents for my men, and had intended that they should sleep with Ibbotson's men in the outbuildings of the Inspection Bungalow, but this they had refused to do, asserting that there was no more danger for them than there was for me in the open tent. My cook—who was, I discovered, a very noisy sleeper—was lying next to and about a yard from me, and beyond him, packed like sardines in the little enclosure, were the six Garhwalis I had brought from Naini Tal.

The weak spot in our defence was the tree, and I went to sleep thinking of it.

It was a brilliant moonlit night, and round about midnight I was suddenly awakened by hearing the leopard climbing the tree. Picking up the riffle, which was lying ready loaded on the bed, I swung my legs off the bed and had just slipped my feet into my slippers—to avoid the thorns which were scattered all round—when there was an ominous crack from the partly-cut-through tree, followed by a yell from the cook of 'Bagh! Baghl' In one jump I was outside the tent and, swinging round, was just too late to get the rifle to bear on the leopard as it sprang up the bank on to a terraced field. Pulling the bush out of the gap I dashed up to the field which was about forty yards in width and bare of crops, and as I stood scanning the hillside dotted over with thornbushes and a few big rocks, the alarm call of a jackal far up the hill informed me that the leopard had ' gone beyond my reach.

The cook informed me later that he had been lying on his back—a fact of which I had long been aware—and hearing the tree crack he had opened his eyes and looked straight into the leopard's face just as it was preparing to jump down.

The tree was cut down next day and the fence strengthened, and though we stayed in that camp for several weeks our slumbers were not again disturbed.

THE GIN-TRAP

From reports received from nearby villages where unsuccessful attempts had been made to break into houses, and from the pugmarks I had seen on the roads, I knew that the man-eater was still in the vicinity, and a few days after the arrival of the Ibbotsons, news was brought that a cow had been killed in a village two miles from Rudraprayag, and about half a mile from the village where I had sat on the hayrick in a walnut tree.

Arrived at the village we found that a leopard had broken down the door of a one-roomed house and had killed and dragged to the door one of the several cows that were in it, and not being able to drag it through the door, had left it on the threshold after eating a good meal.

The house was in the heart of the village, and on prospecting round, we found that by making a hole in the wall of a house a few yards away we could overlook the kill.

The owner of this house, who was also the owner of the dead cow, was only too willing to fall in with our plans, and as evening closed in we locked ourselves very securely into the room, and after eating our sandwiches and drinking the tea we had brought with us, we mounted guard in turns over the hole in the wall throughout the long night without either seeing or hearing anything of the leopard.

When we emerged in the morning the villagers took us round the village, which was of considerable size, and showed us the claw-marks on doors and windows made by the man-eater in the course of years, in his attempts to get at the inmates. One door in particular had more and deeper claw-marks than any other—it was the door the leopard had forced to enter the room in which the forty goats and the boy had been secured.

A day or two later another cow was reported to have been killed in a small village on the hill a few hundred yards from the bungalow. Here again we found that the cow had been killed inside a house, dragged as far as the door, and partly eaten. Facing the door, and distant from it about ten yards, was a newly built hayrick, sixteen feet tall and built on a wooden platform two feet above ground.

News of the kill was brought to us early in the morning, so we had the whole day before us, and the *machan* we built by evening was I am sure not only the most effective, but also the most artistic, that has ever been .' constructed for a similar purpose.

To start with, the rick was dismantled, and a scaffolding of poles was set round the platform. With these poles to support it, a second, and smaller, platform was built four feet above the lower one. Two-inch-mesh wire-netting was then wound round the whole structure, leaving only the space bare between the lower platform and the ground. Wisps of straw were then looped into the meshes of the netting, and a little straw was spread round the rick and under the platform, just as it had been before we started work. One of the joint owners of the hayrick, who had been absent from the village for a day or two and.who returned just as we had finished our task, would not believe that the rick had been disturbed until he felt it all round, and had been shown the second rick we had built with the spare hay in an adjoining field.

As the sun was setting we crawled through the hole we had left in the netting and entered the *machan*, securely closing the entrance behind us. Ibbotson is a little shorter than me, so he took the upper platform, and when we had made ourselves comfortable we each made a small hole in the straw to shoot through. As it would not be possible for us to communicate with each other once the leopard arrived, we agreed that whoever saw it first was to fire. It was a bright moonlit night, so there was no need for either of us to use the electric light.

Sounds in the village quietened down after the evening meal had been eaten, and at about 10 p.m. I heard the leopard coming down the hill behind us. On arriving at the rick it paused for a few minutes and then started to crawl under the platform I was sitting on. Immediately below me, and with only the thickness of a plank between my seat and his head, he paused for a long minute and then started to crawl forward; and just as I was expecting him to emerge from under the platform and give me an easy shot at a range of three or four feet, there was a loud creak in the platform above me. The leopard dashed out to the right, where I could not see him, and went up the hill. The creaking of the planks at the critical moment had resulted from Ibbotson changing his position to relieve a very painful cramp in both legs. After the fright he had got, the leopard abandoned the kill and did not return that night, or the next night.

Two nights later another cow was killed a few hundred yards above the Rudraprayag bazaar.

The owner of this cow lived alone in an isolated house which contained only one room, a room which was divided by a rough partition made of odd bits of plank into a kitchen and living-room. Sometime during the night a noise in the kitchen—the door of which he had forgotten to shut—-awakened the man, and a little later, in the dim moonlight which the open door was admitting, he saw the leopard through the wide chinks in the partition, trying to tear one of the planks out.

For a long time the man lay and sweated, while the leopard tried plank after plank. Eventually, being unable to find a weak place in the partition, the leopard left the kitchen, and killed the man's cow, which was tethered in a grass lean-to against the side of the house. After killing the cow the leopard broke the rope by which it was tethered, dragged it a short distance from the lean-to, and left it out in the open after partaking of a good meal.

On the very edge of the hill, and about twenty yards from where the dead cow was lying, there was a fair-sized tree, in the upper branches of which a hayrick had been built; on this natural macban—from which there was a sheer drop of several hundred feet into the valley below— Ibbotson and I decided to sit.

To assist in killing the man-eater, the Government a few days previously had sent us a gin-trap. This trap, which was five feet long and weighed eighty pounds, was the most fearsome thing of its kind I have ever seen. Its jaws, armed with sharp teeth three inches long, had a spread of twenty-four inches, and were actuated by two powerful springs, which needed two men to compress.

When leaving the kill the leopard had followed a footpath across a field about forty yards wide, up a three-foot bank, and across another field bordered by a densely scrub-covered hill. At this three-foot step from the upper to the lower field, we set the trap, and to ensure the leopard stepping on to it we planted a few thorn twigs on either side of the path. To one of the traps was attached a short length of half-inch-thick chain, terminating in a ring three inches in diameter; through this ring we drove a stout peg, chaining the trap to the ground.

When these arrangements had been completed, Jean Ibbotson returned to the bungalow with our men, and Ibbotson and I climbed up to the hayrick. After tying a stick in front of us and looping a little hay over it, to act as a screen, we made ourselves comfortable, and waited for the leopard, which we felt sure would not escape us on this occasion.

As evening closed in heavy clouds spread over the sky, and as the moon was not due to rise until 9 p.m., we had of necessity to depend on the electric light for the accuracy of our shooting until then. This light was a heavy and cumbersome affair, and as Ibbotson insisted on my taking the shot, I attached it to my rifle with some little difficulty.

An hour after dark a succession of angry roars apprised us of the fact that the leopard was in the trap. Switching on the electric light, I saw the leopard rearing up with the trap dangling from his forelegs, and taking a hurried shot, my .450 bullet struck a link in the chain and severed it.

Freed from the peg the leopard went along the field in a series of great leaps, carrying the trap in front of him, followed up by the bullet from my left barrel, and two lethal bullets from Ibbotson's shotgun, all of which missed him. In trying to reload my rifle I displaced some part of the light, after which it refused to function.

Hearing the roars of the leopard and our four shots, the people in Rudraprayag bazaar, and in nearby villages, swarmed out of their houses carrying lanterns and pinetorches, and converged from all sides on the isolated house. Shouting to them to keep clear was of no avail, for they were making so much noise that they could not hear us; so while I climbed down the tree, taking my rifle with me—a hazardous proceeding in the dark—Ibbotson lit and pumped up the petrol lamp we had taken into the *machan* with us. Letting the lamp down to me on the end of a length of rope, Ibbotson joined me on the ground, and together we went in the direction the leopard had taken. Halfway along the field there was a hump caused by an outcrop of rock; this hump we approached, with Ibbotson holding the heavy lamp high above his head, while I walked by his side with rifle to shoulder. Beyond the hump was a little depression, and crouching down in this depression and facing us and growling, was the leopard. Within a few minutes of my bullet crashing into his head, we were surrounded by an excited crowd, who literally danced with joy round their long-dreaded enemy.

The animal that lay dead before me was an out-sized male leopard, who the previous night had tried to tear down a partition to get at a human being, and who had been shot in an area in which dozens of human beings had been killed, all good and sufficient reasons for assuming that he was the man-eater. But I could not make myself believe that he was the same animal I had seen the night I sat over the body of the woman. True, it had been a dark night and I had only vaguely seen the outline of the leopard; even so, I was convinced that the animal that was now being lashed to a pole by willing hands was not the man-eater.

With the Ibbotsons leading the way, followed by the men carrying the leopard and a crowd of several hundred men, we set off via the bazaar for the bungalow.

As I stumbled down the hill in the wake of the procession—the only one in all that throng who did not believe that the man-eating leopard of Rudraprayag was dead—my thoughts went back to an occurrence that had taken place not far from our winter home when

I was a small boy, and which I saw recounted many years later in a book entitled Brave Deeds, or perhaps it was Bravest Deeds. The occurence concerned two men: Smeaton of the Indian Civil Service and Braidwood of the Forest Department. One dark stormy night, in pre-railway days, these two men were travelling in a dak-gharry from Moradabad to Kaladhungi, and on going round a bend in the road they ran into a rogue elephant. In killing the driver and the two horses, the elephant overturned the gharry. Braidwood had a rifle, and while he got it out of its case, put it together, and loaded it, Smeaton climbed on to the gharry and released the one unbroken lamp from its socket. Then Smeaton, holding the oil lamp which only gave a glimmer of light over his head, advanced up to the elephant and shone the light on his forehead, to enable Braidwood to get in a killing shot. Admittedly there was a great difference between a rogue elephant and a leopard; even so, there are few who would care to walk up to a pain-maddened leopard— which we later found had practically torn its paw free and was only held by a thin strip of skin—holding a lamp above his head and depending for safety on a companion's bullet.

For the first night in many years every house in the bazaar was open, with women and children standing in the doorways. Progress was slow, for every few yards the leopard was put down to let the children cluster round and get a better view of it. At the farther end of the long street our escort left us, and the leopard was carried in triumph to the bungalow by our men.

Returning to the bungalow after a wash at my camp, the Ibbotsons and I, both during and long after it, put forward our arguments for and against the dead leopard being the man-eater. Eventually, without either side convincing the other, we decided that as Ibbotson had to get back to his work at Pauri, and I was tired out after my long stay at Rudraprayag, we would spend the next day in skinning the leopard and drying the skin, and on the day after would break camp and make for Pauri.

From early morning to late evening, relays of men kept coming in from near and distant villages to see the leopard, and as most of these men asserted that they recognized the animal as the man-eater, the conviction of the Ibbotsons, that they were right and I was wrong, grew. Two concessions at my request Ibbotson made: he added his warning to the people to mind, not to relax precautions against the man-eater, and he refrained from telegraphing to tell the Government that we had shot the man-eater.

We went early to bed that night, for we were to start at daybreak next morning. I was up while it was still dark and was having chota hazri when I heard voices on the road. As this was very unusual, I called out to ask what men were doing on the road at that hour. On seeing me, four men climbed up the path to my camp, and informed me they had been sent by the *patwari* to tell me that a woman had been killed by the man-eater on the far side of the river, about a mile from the Chatwapipal bridge.

THE HUNTERS HUNTED

Ibbotson was just unbolting the door to admit his man with early tea when I arrived, and after he had countermanded his move to Pauri we sat on Jean's bed with a large-scale map between us, drinking tea and discussing our plans.

Ibbotson's work at his headquarters at Pauri was pressing, and at most he could only spare two more days and nights. I had telegraphed to Naini Tal the previous day to say I was returning home via Pauri and Kotdwara; this telegram I decided to cancel, and instead of going by rail, I would return on foot the way I had come. These details settled, and the village where the woman had been killed found on the map, I returned to camp to tell my men of our change of plans, and to instruct them to pack up and follow us, accompanied by the four men who had brought news of the kill.

Jean was to remain at Rudraprayag, so after breakfast Ibbotson and I set off on two of his horses, a Gulf Arab and an English mare, two of the most surefooted animals I have ever had the good fortune to ride.

We took our rifles, a blue-flame stove, a petrol-lamp, and some provisions with us, and were accompanied by one of Ibbotson's syces on a borrowed horse, carrying food for our horses.

We left the horses at the Chatwapipal bridge. This bridge had not been closed the night we shot the leopard, with the result that the man-eater had got across the river and secured a kill at the first village he visited.

A guide was waiting for us at the bridge, and he took us up a very steep ridge and along a grassy hillside, and then down into a deep and densely wooded ravine with a small stream flowing through it. Here we found the *patwari* and some twenty men guarding the kill.

The kill was a very robust and fair girl, some eighteen or twenty years of age. She was lying on her face with her hands by her sides. Every vestige of clothing had been stripped from her, and she had been licked by the leopard from the soles of her feet to her neck, in which were four great teeth-marks; only a few pounds of flesh had been eaten from the upper portion of her body, and a few pounds from the lower portion.

The drums we had heard as we came up the hill were being beaten by the men who were guarding the kill, and as it was then about 2 p.m. and there was no chance of the leopard being anywhere in the vicinity, we went up to the village to brew ourselves some tea, taking the *patwari* and the guard with us.

After tea we went and had a look at the house where the girl had been killed. It was a stone-built house, consisting of one room, situated in the midst of terraced fields some two or three acres in extent, and it was occupied by the girl, her husband, and their six-month-old child.

Two days previous to the kill, the husband had gone to Pauri to give evidence in a land dispute case, and had left his father in charge of the house. On the night of the kill, after the girl and her father-in-law had partaken of their evening meal and it was getting near time to retire for the night, the girl, who had been nursing her child, handed it over to her father-in-law, unlatched the door, and stepped outside to squat down—I have already mentioned that there are no sanitary conveniences in the houses of our hill-folk.

When the child was transferred from the mother to the grandfather, it started crying, so even if there had been any sound from outside—and I am sure there was none—he would not have heard it. It was a dark night. After waiting for a few minutes the man called to the girl; and receiving no answer he called again. Then he got up and hurriedly closed and latched the door.

Rain had fallen earlier in the evening and it was easy to reconstruct the scene. Shortly after the rain had stopped, the leopard, coming from the direction of the village, had crouched down behind a rock in the field, about thirty yards to the left front of the door.

Here it had lain for some time—possibly listening to the man and the girl talking. When the girl opened door she squatted down on its right-hand side, partly turning her back on the leopard, who had crept round the far side of the rock, covered the twenty yards separating him from the corner of the house with belly to ground and, creeping along close to the wall of the house, had caught the girl from behind, and dragged her to the rock. Here, when the girl was dead, or possibly when the man called out in alarm, the leopard had picked her up and, holding her high, so that no mark of hand or foot showed on the soft newly ploughed ground, had carried her across one field, down a three-foot bank, and across another field which ended in a twelve-foot drop on to a well-used footpath. Down this drop the leopard had sprung with the girl—who weighed about eleven stone—in his mouth, and some idea of his strength will be realized from the fact that when he landed on the footpath he did not let any portion of her body come in contact with the ground.

Crossing the footpath he had gone straight down the hill for half a mile, to the spot where he had undressed the girl. After eating a little of her, he had left her lying in a little glade of emerald-green grass, under the shade of a tree roofed over with dense creepers.

At about four o'clock we went down to sit over the kill, taking the petrol-lamp and night-shooting light with us.

It was reasonable to assume that the leopard had heard the noise the villagers made when searching for the girl, and later when guarding the body, and that if it returned to the kill it would do so with great caution; so we decided not to sit near the kill, and selected a tree about sixty yards away on the hill overlooking the glade.

This tree, a stunted oak, was growing out of the hill at almost a right angle, and after we had hidden the petrol-lamp in a little hollow and covered it over with pine-needles, Ibbotson took his seat in a fork of the tree from where he had a clear view of the kill, while I sat on the trunk with my back to him and facing the hill; Ibbotson was to take the shot, while I saw to our safety. As the shooting light was not functioning— possibly because the battery had faded out—our plan was to sit up as long as Ibbotson could see to shoot and then, with the help of the petrol-lamp, get back to the village where we hoped to find that our men had arrived from Rudraprayag.

We had not had time to prospect the ground, but the villagers had informed us that there was heavy jungle to the east of the kill, to which they felt sure the leopard had retired when they drove it off. If the leopard came from this direction, Ibbotson would see it long before it got to the glade and would get an easy shot, for his rifle was fitted with a telescopic sight which not only made for accurate shooting, but which also gave us an extra half-hour, as we had found from tests. When a minute of daylight more or less may make the difference between success and failure, this modification of the light factor is very important.

The sun was setting behind the high hills to the west, and we had been in shadow for some minutes when a *kakar* dashed down the hill, barking, from the direction in which we had been told there was heavy jungle. On the shoulder of the hill the animal pulled up, and after barking in one spot for some time went away on the far side, and the sound died away in the distance.

The *kakar* had undoubtedly been alarmed by a leopard, and though it was quite possible that there were other leopards in that area, my hopes had been raised, and when I looked round at Ibbotson I saw that he too was keyed up, and that he had both hands on his rifle.

Light was beginning to fade, but was good enough to shoot by even without the aid of the telescopic sight, when a pine-cone dislodged from behind some low bushes thirty yards above us came rolling down the hill and struck the tree close to my feet. The leopard had arrived and, possibly suspecting danger, had taken a line that would enable him to prospect from a safe place on the hill all the ground in the vicinity of his kill. Unfortunately, in so doing he had got our tree in a direct line with the kill, and though I, who was showing no outline, might escape observation, he would be certain to see Ibbotson, who was sitting in a fork of the tree.

When sufficient light for me to shoot by had long since gone, and Ibbotson's telescopic sight was no longer of any use to him, we heard the leopard coming stealthily down towards the tree. It was then time to take action, so I asked Ibbotson to take my place, while I retrieved the lamp. This lamp was of German make and was called a petromax. It gave a brilliant light but, with its long body and longer handle, was not designed to be used as a lantern in a jungle.

I am a little taller than Ibbotson, and suggested that I should carry the lamp, but Ibbotson said he could manage all right, and, moreover, that he would rather depend on my rifle than his own. So we set off, Ibbotson leading and I following with both hands on my rifle.

Fifty yards from the tree, while climbing over a rock, Ibbotson slipped, the base of the lamp came in violent contact with the rock, and the mantle fell in dust to the bottom of the lamp. The streak of blue flame directed from the nozzle on to the petrol reservoir gave sufficient light for us to see where to put our feet, but the question was how long we should have even this much light. Ibbotson was of the opinion that he could carry the lamp for three minutes before it burst. Three minutes, in which to do a stiff climb of half a mile, over ground on which it was necessary to change direction every few steps to avoid huge rocks and thornbushes, and possibly followed—and actually followed as we found later—by a man-eater, was a terrifying prospect.

There are events in one's life which, no matter how remote, never fade from memory; the climb up that hill in the dark was for me one of them. When we eventually reached the footpath our troubles were not ended, for the path was a series of buffalo wallows, and we did not know where our men were. Alternately slipping on wet ground and stumbling over unseen rocks, we at last came to some stone steps which took off from the path and went up to the right. Climbing these steps we found a small courtyard, on the far side of which was a door. We had heard the gurgling of a hookah as we came up the steps, so I kicked the door and shouted to the inmates to open. As no answer came, I took out a box of matches and shook it, crying that if the door was not opened in a minute I would set the thatch alight. On this an agitated voice came from inside the house, begging me not to set the house on fire, and saying that the door was being opened—a minute later first the inner door and then the outer door were opened, and in two strides Ibbotson and I were in the house, slamming the inner door, and putting our backs to it.

There were some twelve or fourteen men, women, and children of all ages in the room. When the men had regained their wits after the unceremonious entry, they begged us to forgive them for not having opened the doors sooner, adding that they and their families had lived so long in terror of the man-eater that their courage had gone. Not knowing what form the man-eater might take, they suspected every sound they heard at night. In their fear they had our full sympathy, for from the time Ibbotson had slipped and broken the mantle, and a few minutes later had extinguished the red-hot lamp to prevent it bursting, I had been convinced that one, and possibly both, of us would not live to reach the village.

We were told that our men had arrived about sundown, and that they had been housed in a block of buildings farther along the hill. The two able-bodied men in the room offered to show us the way, but as we knew it would be murder to let them return to their homes alone, we declined their offer—which had been made with the full realization of the risk it would entail—and asked if they could provide us with a light of some kind. After rummaging about in a corner of the room, an old and decrepit lantern with a cracked globe was produced, and when vigorous shaking had revealed that it contained a few drops of oil, it was lit, and with the combined good wishes of the inmates we left the house—the two doors being shut and bolted on our heels.

More buffalo wallows and more sunken rocks, but with the glimmer of light to help us we made good progress and, finding the second lot of steps we had been instructed to climb, we mounted them and found ourselves in a long courtyard facing a row of double-storied buildings extending to the right and to the left, every door of which was fast shut, and not a glimmer of light showing anywhere.

When we called a door was opened, and by climbing a short flight of .'stone steps we gained the verandah of the upper story, and found the two adjoining rooms which had been placed at the disposal of our men and ourselves. While the men were relieving us of the lamp and our rifles, a dog arrived from nowhere. He was just a friendly village pye, and after sniffing round our legs and wagging his tail, he went towards the steps up which we had just come. The next second, with a scream of fear followed by hysterical barking, he backed towards us with all his hair on end.

The lantern we had been lent had died on us as we reached the courtyard, but our men had procured its twin brother. Though Ibbotson held it at all angles while I hurriedly reloaded my rifle, he could not get its light to illuminate the ground eight feet below.

By watching the dog it was possible to follow the movements of the leopard. When the leopard had crossed the yard and gone down the steps leading to the footpath, the dog gradually stopped barking and lay down intently watching in that direction, and growling at intervals.

Ihe room that had been vacated for us had no windows, and as the only way in which we could have occupied it in safety would have been by closing the solid door, and excluding all air and light, we decided to spend the night on the verandah. The dog evidently belonged to the late occupant of the room and had been accustomed to sleeping there, for he lay contentedly at our feet and gave us a feeling of safety as we watched in turn through the long hours of the night.

RETREAT

At daybreak next morning we very carefully stalked the kill, and were disappointed to find that the leopard had not returned to it, which we felt sure he would do after his failure to bag one of us the previous evening.

During the day, while Ibbotson dealt with some office work that had been sent out to him, I took a rifle and went off to see if I could get a shot at the leopard. Tracking on the hard and pine-needle-covered ground was not possible, so I made for the shoulder of the hill beyond which the villagers had told us there was heavy jungle. Here I found the ground very difficult to negotiate, for, in addition to dense scrub jungle through which it was not possible to penetrate, there was a series of rock cliffs on which it was impossible for a human being to find foothold. In this area there was a surprisingly large head of game, and on the paths that intersected it I found the tracks of *kakar*, ghooral, pig, and a solitary sarao. Of the leopard—except for a few old scratch-marks—I found no trace.

The gin-trap that had been sent off from Rudraprayag the previous day arrived while we were having lunch, and in the early evening we took it down to the glade and, after setting it, poisoned the kill with cyanide. I had no experience of poisons, nor had Ibbotson, but in a conversation with a doctor friend before leaving Naini Tal I had mentioned that Government wanted me to try every means to kill the man-eater, and that there was little use in my trying poison, as the records showed that the leopard throve on it. I told him what poisons had hitherto been tried, and he then recommended my using cyanide, which was the best poison for the cat family. I had passed this information on to Ibbotson, and a few days previously a supply had arrived, with capsules with which to use it. We inserted a few of these capsules in the kill at the places where the leopard had eaten.

There was every hope of the leopard returning to the kill this second night, and as he had seen us on the tree the previous evening we decided not to sit up, but to leave him to the gin-trap and to the poison.

In a big pine-tree near the footpath we built a *machan*, which we padded with hay and on which we took up our position after we had eaten the dinner which Ibbotson cooked on the blue-flame stove. Here on the comfortable *machan* we were able to lie at full stretch and talk and smoke, for our only reason for being there was to listen for sounds from the direction of the kill. We watched and slept by turns, hoping to hear the angry roar of the leopard if by accident it walked into the trap, for here there was no well-used track along which to direct the leopard to it.

Once during the night a *kakar* barked, but in the opposite direction to that from which we expected the leopard to come.

At the first streak of dawn we climbed out of the tree and, after brewing purselves a cup of tea, visited the kill, which we found lying just as we had left it.

Ibbotson left for Rudraprayag after an early breakfast, and I was packing my things and having a final word with the villagers before starting on my fifteen-day journey back to Naini Tal when a party of men arrived to give the news that a cow had been killed by a leopard in a village four miles away. They suspected that the cow had been killed by the man-eater, for the previous night—the night the leopard had followed Ibbotson and myself from the tree to the verandah—and towards the small hours of the morning, the leopard had made a determined attempt to break down the door of the Headman's house; late the following evening, the cow had been killed in the jungle three hundred yards from this house. At the urgent request of these men I postponed my departure to Naini Tal and accompanied them back to their village, taking the gin-trap and a supply of poison with me.

The Headman's house was on a little knoll surrounded by cultivated land, and was approached by a footpath which for a short distance ran over soft and boggy ground; here I found the pugmarks of the man- eater.

The Headman had seen me approaching across the valley and had a steaming dish of tea brewed in fresh milk and sweetened with jaggery, waiting for me. While I drank this rich and over-sweetened liquid on the courtyard, sitting on a reed couch upholstered with ghooral skins, he drew my attention to the condition of the door which two nights previously the leopard had attempted to break down, in which attempt it would undoubtedly have succeeded if he had not fortunately had some sawn timber in the house—-intended for repairing the roof—which he had used to shore up the door from inside.

The Headman was old and crippled with rheumatism, so he sent his son to show me the kill while he made room in the house for myself and my men.

I found the kill—a young cow in grand condition—lying on a flat bit of ground just above the cattle track, in an ideal position for setting up the gin-trap. Its back was against a tangle of wild rose-bushes, and its hooves were against a foot-high bank; while eating, the leopard had sat on the bank with its forepaws between the cow's legs.

Having dug away the ground between the cows legs and removed it to a distance, I set the trap where the leopard had placed his paws and covered it over with big green leaves. Then, after sprinkling on a layer of earth, I replaced the deal leaves, bits of dry sticks, and splinters of bone in the exact position between the cow's legs in which I had found them. Not one of a hundred human beings going to the kill would have noticed that the ground had in any way been disturbed, and a deadly trap set.

My arrangements made to my satisfaction I retraced my steps and climbed a tree halfway between the kill and the Headman's house, where I would be handy if needed at the trap.

Near sundown a pair of *kalege* pheasants and their brood of five chicks, which I had been watching for some time, suddenly took alarm and went scuttling down the hill, and a few seconds later a *kakar* came dashing towards me and after barking under my tree for a little while, went off up the hill on tiptoe. Nothing happened after that, and when it was getting too dark under the shade of the trees for me to see the sights of my rifle, I slipped off the tree and myself tiptoed away on rubber-shod feet towards the village.

A hundred yards from the Headman's house the track ran across an open glade, some thirty yards long and twenty yards wide. On the upper, hill side of the glade was a big rock. As I reached this open ground I felt I was being followed, and, determined to exploit the situation, I left the track and, taking two long steps over soft and spongy ground, lay down behind the rock, with only one eye showing in the direction of the kill.

For ten minutes I lay on the wet ground. When daylight had all but gone I regained the path and, taking every precaution, covered the remaining distance to the Headman's house.

Once during the night the Headman roused me from a sound sleep to tell me he had heard the leopard scratching on the door, and when I opened the door next morning I saw the pugmarks of the man-eater in the dust in front of it. These pugmarks I followed back to the glade, and found that the leopard had done just what I had done the previous evening. He had left the track where I had; had crossed the soft ground to the rock and, after regaining the track, had followed me to the house, •round which he had walked several times.

On leaving the house the leopard had gone back along the track, and as I followed his pugmarks towards the kill my hopes rose high, for up to that time I had not fully realized the degree of cunning that a man-eating leopard can acquire after eight years of close association with human beings.

I left the track and approached from the high ground, and from a little distance away saw that the kill had gone, and that the ground where the trap had been buried was, except for two pugmarks, undisturbed.

Sitting on the foot-high bank, as he had done the first night, the leopard had put both front paws between the cow's legs, but on this occasion he had spread them wide apart and rested them on the buried levers of the trap which, released, would have closed the great jaws. Here, safe from the trap, he had eaten his meal, and when he had done, he skirted round the flat ground and, getting hold of the cow by the head, had dragged it through the rose-thorns and rolled it down the hill, where fifty yards lower down it had fetched up against an oak sapling. Content with his nights work, the leopard had then gone along the cattle track, and after following him for a mile I lost his tracks on hard ground.

There was no hope of the leopard returning to the kill. However, to salve my conscience for not having done so the previous night, I put a liberal dose of cyanide in the carcass of the cow. Truth to tell I hated the very thought of using poison then, and I hate it no less now.

I visited the kill in the morning and found that a leopard had eaten all that portion of the cow that I had poisoned. So sure was I that the poison had been eaten by a leopard that had accidentally come across the kill, and not by the man-eater, that on my return to the village I told the Headman that I would not stay to recover the leopard, though I would pay a hundred rupees to anyone who found it and took its skin to the pativari. A month later the reward was claimed, and the skin of a leopard which had been dead many days was buried by the *patwari*.

It did not take my men long to pack up, and shortly after midday we started on our long journey back to Naini Tal. As we went down a narrow footpath to the Chatwapipal bridge a big rat snake leisurely crossed the path, and as I stood and watched it slip away Madho Singh, who was behind me, said, 'There goes the evil spirit that has been responsible for your failure.'

My action in leaving Garhwal to the tender mercies of the man-eater may appear heartless to you—it did so to me—and was adversely criticized in the press, for the leopard at that time was daily mentioned in the Indian papers. Ip extenuation I would urge that an effort entailing great strain cannot be indefinitely sustained. There were twenty-four hours in every day of the many weeks I spent in Garhwal, and time and time again after sitting up all night, I walked endless miles next day, visiting distant villages from which reports had come of unsuccessful attacks by the man-eater. On many moonlit nights, when sitting in an uncomfortable position physical endurance had reached its limit, and when sitting where it would have been easy for the leopard to have got at me I had no longer been able to keep my eyes open. I had for hours walked the roads which were alone open to me and to the leopard, trying every trick I knew of to outwit my adversary, and the man-eater had, with luck beyond his deserts or with devilish cunning, avoided the bullet that a press of my finger would have sent into him, for on retracing my steps in the morning after these night excursions I had found from the pugmarks on the road that I was right in assuming I had been closely followed. To know that one is being followed at night—no matter how bright the moon may be—by a man- eater intent on securing a victim, gives one an inferiority complex that is very unnerving, and that is not mitigated by repetition.

Tired out in mind and in body, my longer stay at Rudraprayag would not have profited the people of Garhwal, and it might have cost me my own life. Knowing that the temporary abandonment of my self-imposed task would be severely criticized by the press, but that what I was now doing was right, I plodded on towards my distant home, having assured the people of Garhwal that I would return to help them as soon as it was possible for me to do so.

FISHING INTERLUDE

I left the scene of my failure, weary and dispirited, in the late autumn of 1925, and returned to continue my labour, refreshed and full of hope, in the early spring of 1926.

On this my second visit to Garhwal in pursuit of the man-eater, I travelled by train to Kotdwara and went from there by foot to Pauri, thus saving eight days on the journey. At Pauri, Ibbotson joined me and accompanied me to Rudraprayag.

During my three months' absence from Garhwal the man-eater had killed ten human beings, and during these three months no attempt had been made by the terror-stricken inhabitants to kill the leopard.

The last of these ten kills—the victim was a small boy—had taken place on the left bank of the Alaknanda, two days before our arrival at Rudraprayag. We had received telegraphic news of this kill at Pauri, and though we had travelled as fast as it was possible for us to do, we were disappointed to learn from the *patwari*, who was awaiting our arrival at the Inspection Bungalow, that the leopard disposed of the entire kill the previous night, leaving nothing of its small victim over which we could sit.

The boy had been killed at midnight in a village four miles from Rudraprayag, and as it was unlikely that the leopard had crossed the river after his undisturbed feed, we took steps immediately on our arrival to close the two suspension bridges.

During the winter Ibbotson had organized a very efficient intelligence service throughout the area in which the man-eater was operating. If in this area a dog, goat, cow, or human being was killed, or an attempt made to force open a door, news of the occurrence was conveyed to us by the service, and in this way we were able to keep in constant touch with the man-eater. Hundreds of false rumours of alleged attacks by the man-eater were brought to us, entailing endless miles of walking, but this was only to be expected, for in an area in which an established man-eater is operating everyone suspects their own shadows, and every sound heard at night is attributed to the man-eater.

One of these rumours concerned a man by the name of Galtu, a resident of Kunda, a village seven miles from Rudraprayag on the right bank of the Alaknanda. Galtu left the village in the evening to spend the night in his cattle shed a mile away from the village, and when his son went to the shed next morning he found his father's blanket half in and half out of the door of the shed, and in a patch of soft ground nearby he found what he thought was drag mark, and near it the pugmarks of the man-eater. Returning to the village he raised an alarm, and while sixty men went off to search for the body, four men were dispatched to Rudraprayag to inform us. Ibbotson and I were beating a hillside on the left bank of the river for the man-eater when the men arrived, and as I was convinced that the leopard was on our side of the river, and that there was no truth in the rumour that Galtu had been killed, Ibbotson sent a *patwari* back to Kunda with the four men, with instructions to make a personal search and report back to us. Next evening we received the*patwari*'s report, with a sketch of the pugmarks in the soft earth near the door of the shed. The report stated that an all-day search of the surrounding country, with two hundred men, had not resulted in finding Galtu's remains, and that the search would be continued. The sketch showed six circles, the inner one as large as a plate, with five equally spaced circles round it, each the size of a tea cup; all the circles had been made with a compass. Five days later, and just as Ibbotson and I were setting out to sit up on the tower of the bridge, a procession came up to the bungalow led by an irate man who was protesting loudly that he had committed no offence that justified his being arrested and brought to Rudraprayag. The irate man was Galtu. After we had pacified him, he gave us his story. It appeared that just as he was leaving his house on the night he was alleged to have been carried off by the man-eater, his son arrived and informed him that he had paid Rs 100 for a pair of bullocks which Galtu asserted were not worth more than Rs 70. The wanton waste of good money had so angered him that, after sleeping the night in the cattle shed, he had got up early next morning and gone to a village ten miles away, where a married daughter of his was living. On his return to his village that morning, he had been arrested by the *patwari*, and he wanted to know what crime he had committed that justified his arrest. It was some little time before he saw the humour of the situation, but once having done so, he laughed as heartily as any of the assembled throng at the thought of an important person like a *patwari*, and two hundred of his friends, searching for five days for his remains, what time he was cooling off in a village ten miles away.

Ibbotson was averse to lying all night on the wind-swept tower of the Rudraprayag suspension bridge, and as wood and carpenters were available, he had a platform built in the arch of the tower, and on this platform we sat for the five nights Ibbotson was able to spend at Rudraprayag.

After Ibbotson's departure the leopard killed one dog, four goats, and two cows. The dog and goats had been eaten out on the nights on which they had been killed, but I sat over each of the cows for two nights. On the second night on which I was sitting up over the first cow, the leopard came, but just as I was raising my rifle and preparing to switch on the torch I had provided myself with, a woman in the house adjoining the one I was sitting in, thumped on the door preparatory to opening it, and unfortunately frightened the leopard away.

No human beings had been killed during this period, but a woman and her baby had been badly mauled. The leopard had forced open the door of the room in which she was sleeping with her baby, and seizing her arm had attempted to drag her out of the room. The woman fortunately was stout of heart, and had not fainted or lost her wits, and after the leopard—dragging her along the floor—had backed out of the room, she shut the door on it, and escaped with a badly lacerated arm and several deep wounds on her breast, while the baby escaped with one head wound. I sat in this room for the following two nights, but the leopard did not return.

I was returning one day towards the latter end of March, after visiting a village on the Kedarnath pilgrim route, when, as I approached a spot where the road runs close alongside the Mandakini river, and where there is a waterfall ten to twelve feet high, I saw a number of men sitting on the rock at the head of the fall on the far side of the river, armed with a triangular net attached to a long bamboo pole. The roar of the water prevented conversation, so leaving the road I sat down on the rocks on my side of the fall, to have a rest and a smoke—for I had walked for that day—and to see what the men were doing.

Presently one of the men got to his feet, and as he pointed down excitedly into the foaming white water at the foot of the fall, two of his companions manning the long pole held the triangular net close to the fall. A large shoal of *mahseer* fish, varying in size from five to fifty pounds, were attempting to leap the fall. One of these fish, about ten pounds in weight, leapt clear of the fall and when falling back was expertly caught in the net. After the fish had been extracted and placed in a basket, the net was again held out close to the fall. I watched the sport for about an hour,

during which time the men caught four fish, all about the same size—ten pounds.

On my previous visit to Rudraprayag I had been informed by the *chowkidar* in charge of the Inspection Bungalow that there was good fishing in the spring—before the snow-water came down—in both the Alaknanda and Mandakini rivers, so I had come armed on this my second visit with a fourteen-foot split cane salmon rod, a silex reel with two hundred and fifty yards of line, a few stout traces, and an assortment of home-made brass spoons varying in size from one to two inches.

The following morning—as no news had come in of the man-eater—I set off for the waterfall with my rod and tackle.

No fish were leaping the fall as they had been doing the previous day, and the men on the far side of the river were sitting in a group round a small fire smoking a hookah which was passing from hand to hand. They watched me with interest.

Below the waterfall was a pool thirty to forty yards wide, flanked on both sides by a wall of rock, and about two hundred yards long, one hundred yards of which was visible from where I stood at the head of the pool. The water in this beautiful and imposing pool was crystal-clear.

The rock face at the head of the pool rose sheer up out of the water to a height of twelve feet, and after keeping at this height for twenty yards, sloped gradually upwards to a height of a hundred feet. It was not possible to get down to water level anywhere on my side of the pool, nor would it be possible, or profitable, to follow a fish—assuming that I hooked one— along the bank, for at the top of the high ground there were trees and bushes, and at the tail of the pool the river cascaded down in a foaming torrent to its junction with the Alaknanda. To land a fish in this pool would be a difficult and a hazardous task, but the crossing of that bridge could be deferred until the fish had been hooked—and I had not yet put together my rod.

On my side of the pool the water—shot through with millions of small bubbles—was deep, and from about halfway across a shingle bottom was showing, over which four to six feet of water was flowing. Above this shingle bottom, every stone and pebble of which was visible in the clear water, a number of fish, ranging in size from three to ten pounds, were slowly moving upstream. As I watched these fish, standing on the rocks twelve feet above the water with a two-inch spoon mounted with a single strong treble hook in my hand, a flight of fingerlings flashed out of the deep water and went skimming over the shingle bottom, hotly pursued by three big *mahseer*. Using the good salmon rod as friend Hardy had never intended that it should be used—and as it had been used on many previous occasions—I slung the spoon out, and in my eagerness over-estimated the distance, with the result that the spoon struck the rock on the far side of the pool, about two feet above the water. The falling of the spoon into the water coincided with the arrival of the fingerlings at the rock, and the spoon had hardly touched the water, when it was taken by the leading *mahseer*.

Striking with a long line from an elevated position entails a very heavy strain, but my good rod stood the strain, and the strong treble hook was firmly fixed in the *mahseer*'s mouth. For a moment or two the fish did not appear to realize what had happened as, standing perpendicularly in the water with his white belly towards me, he shook his head from side to side, and then, possibly frightened by the dangling spoon striking against his head, he gave a mighty splash and went tearing downstream, scattering in all directions the smaller fish that were lying on the shingle bottom.

In his first run the *mahseer* ripped a hundred yards of line off the reel, and after a moment's check carried on for another fifty yards. There was plenty of line still on the reel, but the fish had now gone round the bend and was getting dangerously near the tail of the pool. Alternately easing and tightening the strain on the line, I eventually succeeded in turning his head upstream, and having done so, very gently pulled him round the bend, into the hundred yards of water I was overlooking.

Just below me a projection of rock had formed a backwater, and into this backwater the fish, after half an hour's game fight, permitted himself to be drawn.

I had now very definitely reached my bridge and had just regretfully decided that, as there was no way of crossing it, the fish would have to be cut adrift, when a shadow fell across the rock beside me. Peering over the rock into the backwater, the new arrival remarked that it was a very big fish, and in the same breath asked what I was going to do about it. When I told him that it would not be possible to draw the fish up the face of the rock, and that therefore the only thing to do was to cut it free, he said, 'Wait, *sahib*, I will fetch my brother.' His brother—a long and lanky stripling with dancing eyes—had quite evidently been cleaning out a cow shed when summoned, so telling him to go upstream and wash himself lest he should slip on the smooth rock, I held council with the elder man.

Starting from where we were standing, a crack, a few inches wide, ran irregularly down the face of the rock, ending a foot above the water in a ledge some six inches wide. The plan we finally agreed on was that the stripling—Adio presently returned with his arms and legs glistening with water—should go down to the ledge, while the elder brother went down the crack far enough to get hold of the stripling's left hand, while I lay on the rock holding the elder brother's other hand. Before embarking on the plan I asked the brothers whether they knew how to handle a fish and whether they could swim, and received the laughing answer that they had handled fish and swum in the river from childhood.

The snag in the plan was that 1 could not hold the rod and at the same time make a link in the chain. However, some risk had to be taken, so I put the rod down and held the line in my hand, and when the brothers had taken up position I sprawled on the rock and, reaching down, got hold of the elder brother's hand. Then very gently I drew the fish towards the rock, holding the line alternately with my left hand and with my teeth. There was no question that the stripling knew how to handle a fish, for before the fish had touched the rock, he had inserted his thumb into one side of the gills and his fingers into the other, getting a firm grip on the fish's throat. Up to this point the fish had been quite amenable, but on having its throat seized, it lashed out, and for seconds it appeared that the three of us would go headlong into the river.

Both brothers were bare-footed, and when I had been relieved of the necessity of holding the line and was able to help with both hands, they turned and, facing the rock, worked their way up with their toes, while I pulled lustily from on top.

When the fish at last had been safely landed, I asked the brothers if they ate fish, and on receiving their eager answer that they most certainly did, when they could get any, I told them I would give them the fish we had just landed—a *mahseer* in grand condition weighing a little over thirty pounds—if they would help me to land another fish for my men. To this they very readily agreed.

The treble had bitten deep into the leathery underlip of the *mahseer*, and as I cut it out, the brothers watched interestedly. When the hook was free, they asked if they might have a look at it. Three hooks in one, such a thing had never been seen in their village. The bit of bent brass of course acted as a sinker. With what were the hooks baited? Why should fish want to eat brass? And was it really brass, or some kind of hardened bait? When the spoon, and the trace with its three swivels, had been commented on and marvelled at, I made the brothers sit down and watch while I set about catching the second fish.

The biggest fish in the pool were at the foot of the fall, but here in the foaming white water? in addition to *mahseer* were some very big goonch, a fish that takes a spoon of dead bait very readily, and which is responsible for 90 per cent of the tackle lost in our hill rivers through its annoying habit of diving to the bottom of the pool when hooked and getting its head under a rock from where it is always difficult, and often impossible, to dislodge it.

No better spot than the place from where I had made my first cast was available, so here I again took up my position, with rod in hand and spoon held ready for casting.

The fish on the shingle bottom had been disturbed while I was playing the *mahseer* and by our subsequent movements on the face of the rock but were now beginning to return, and presently an exclamation from the brothers, and an excited pointing of fingers, drew my attention to a big fish downstream where the shingle bottom ended and the deep water began. Before I was able to make a cast, the fish turned and disappeared in the deep water, but a little later it reappeared, and as it came into the shallow water I made a cast, but owing to the line being wet the cast fell short. The second cast was beautifully placed and beautifully timed, the spoon striking the water exactly where I wanted it to. Waiting for a second to give the spoon time to sink, I started to wind in the line, giving the spoon just the right amount of spin, and as I drew it along in little jerks, the *mahseer* shot forward, and next moment, with the hook firmly fixed in his mouth, jumped clean out of the water, fell back with a great splash, and went madly downstream, much to the excitement of the spectators, for the men on the far bank had been watching the proceedings as intently as the brothers.

As the reel spun round and the line paid out, the brothers—now standing one on either side of me—urged me not to let the fish go down the run at the trail of the pool. Easier said than done, for it is not possible to stop the first mad rush of a *mahseer* of any size with risking certain break, or the tearing away of the hook-hold. Our luck was in, or else the fish feared the run, for when there was less than fifty yards of line on the reel he checked, and though he continued to fight gamely he was eventually drawn round the bend, and into the little backwater at the foot of the rock.

The landing of this second fish was not as difficult as the landing of the first had been, for we each knew our places on the rock and exactly what to do.

Both fish were the same length, but the second was a little heavier .than the first, and while the elder brother set off in triumph for his village with his fish carried over his shoulder—threaded on a grass cable he had made—the stripling begged to be allowed to accompany me back to the Inspection Bungalow, and to carry both my fish and my rod. Having in the days of long ago been a boy myself, and having had a brother who fished, there was no need for the stripling when making his request to have said, 'If you will let me carry both the fish and the rod, and will walk a little distance behind me, *sahib*, all the people who see me on the road, and in the bazaar, will think that I have caught this great fish, the like of which they have never seen.'

DEATH OF A GOAT

Ibbotson returned from Pauri on the last day of March, and the following morning, while we were having breakfast, we received a report that a leopard had called very persistently the previous night near a village to the north-west of Rudraprayag, about a mile from the place where we had killed the leopard in the gin-trap.

Half a mile to the north of the village, and on the shoulder of the great mountain, there was a considerable area of rough and broken ground where there were enormous rocks and caves, and deep holes in which the locals said their forefathers had quarried copper. Over the whole of this area there was scrub jungle, heavy in some places and light in others, extending down the hillside to within half a mile of the terraced fields above the village.

I had long suspected that the man-eater used this ground as a hide¬out when he was in the vicinity of Rudraprayag, and I had frequently climbed to a commanding position above the broken ground in the hope of finding him basking on the rocks in the early morning sun, for leopards are very fond of doing this in a cold climate, and it is a very common way of shooting them, for all that is needed is a little patience, and accuracy of aim.

After an early lunch Ibbotson and I set out armed with our .275 rifles, and accompanied by one of Ibbotson s men carrying a short length of rope. At the village we purchased a young male goat—the leopard having killed all the goats that I had purchased from time to time.

From the village, a rough goat track ran straight up the hill to the edge of the broken ground, where it turned left, and after running across the face of the hill for a hundred yards carried on round the shoulder of the mountain. The track where it ran across the hill was bordered on the upper side by scattered bushes, and on the steep lower side by short grass.

Having tied the goat to a peg firmly driven into the ground at the bend in the track, about ten yards below the scrub jungle, we went down the hill for a hundred and fifty yards to where there were some big rocks, behind which we concealed ourselves. The goat was one of the best callers I have ever heard, and while his shrill and piercing bleat continued there was no necessity for us to watch him, for he had been very securely tied and there was no possibility of the leopard carrying him away.

The surf—a fiery red ball—was a hand's breadth from the snow mountains above Kedarnath when we took up our position behind the rocks, and half an hour later, when we had been in shadow for a few minutes, the goat suddenly stopped calling. Creeping to the side of the rock and looking through a screen of grass, I saw the goat with ears cocked, looking up towards the bushes; as I watched, the goat shook his head, and backed to the full length of the rope.

The leopard had undoubtedly come, attracted by the calling of the goat, and that he had not pounced before the goat became aware of his presence was proof that he was suspicious. Ibbotson's aim would be more accurate than mine, for his rifle was fitted with a telescopic sight, so I made room for him, and as he lay down and raised his rifle I whispered to him to examine carefully the bushes in the direction in which the goat was looking, for I felt sure that if the goat could see the leopard-—and all the indications were that it could—Ibbotson should also be able to see it through his powerful telescope. For minutes Ibbotson kept his eye to the telescope and then shook his head, laid down the rifle, and made room for me.

The goat was standing in exactly the same position in which I had last seen it, and taking direction from it I fixed the telescope on the same bush at which it was looking. The flicker of an eyelid, or the very least movement of ear or even whiskers, would have been visible through the telescope, but though I also watched for minutes I too could see nothing.

When I took my eye away from the telescope I noted that the light was rapidly fading, and that the goat now showed as a red-and-white blur on the hillside. We had a long way to go and waiting longer would be both useless and dangerous, so getting to my feet I told Ibbotson it was time for us to make a move.

Going up to the goat—who from the time he had stopped bleating had not made a sound—we freed it from the peg, and with the man leading it we set off for the village. The goat quite evidently had never had a rope round its neck before and objected violently to being led, so I told the man to take the rope off—my experience being that when a goat is freed after having been tied up in the jungle, through fear or for want of companionship it follows at heel like a dog. This goat, however, had ideas of its own, and no sooner had the man removed the rope from its neck, than it turned and ran up the track.

It was too good a calling goat to abandon—it had attracted the leopard once, and might do so again. Moreover, we had only a few hours previously paid good money for it, so we in turn ran up the track in hot pursuit. At the bend, the goat turned to the left, and we lost sight of it. Keeping to the track, as the goat had done, we went to the shoulder of the hill where a considerable extent of the hill, clothed in short grass, was visible, and as the goat was nowhere in sight we decided it had taken a short cut back to the village, and started to retrace our steps. I was leading, and as we got halfway along the hundred yards of track, bordered on the upper side by scattered bushes and on the steep lower side by short grass, I saw something white on the track in front of me. The light had nearly gone, and on cautiously approaching the white object I found it was the goat—laid head and tail on the narrow track, in the only position in which it could have been laid to prevent it from rolling down the steep hillside. Blood was oozing from its throat, and when I placed my hand on it the muscles were still twitching.

It was as though the man-eater—for no other leopard would have killed the goat and laid it on the track—had said, 'Here, if you want your goat so badly, take it; and as it is now dark and you have a long way to go, we will see which of you lives to reach the village.'

I do not think all three of us would have reached the village alive if I had not, very fortunately, had a full box of matches with me (Ibbotson at that time was a non-smoker). Striking a match and casting an anxious look all round and taking a few hurried steps, and then again striking another match, we stumbled down the rough track until we got to within calling distance of the village. Then, at our urgent summons, men with lanterns and pine torches came up to meet us.

We had left the goat lying where the leopard had placed it, and when I returned at daybreak next morning I found the pugmarks of the man- eater where he had followed us down to the village, and I found the goat untouched and lying just as we had left it.

CYANIDE POISONING

As I was returning to the Inspection Bungalow after visiting the goat that had been killed the previous night, I was informed in the village that my presence was urgently needed at Rudraprayag, for news had just been received that the man-eater had killed a human being the previous night. My informants were unable to give me any particulars as to where the kill had taken place, but as the pugmarks of the man-eater showed that, after following us to the village, it had gone back up the goat track and turned right at the bend, I assumed—rightly, as I later found—that the leopard, after failing to bag one of us, had secured a victim farther up the mountain-side.

At the bungalow I found Ibbotson in conversation with a man by the name of Nand Ram. Nand Ram's village was about four miles from where we had sat the previous evening. Half a mile above this village and on the far side of a deep ravine, a man of the depressed class, named Gawiya, had cleared a small area of forest land and built himself a house in which he lived with his mother, wife, and three children. At daybreak that morning, Nand Ram had heard the wailing of women from the direction of Gawiya's house and, on his shouting out and asking what was wrong, he had been informed that 'the man of the house' had been carried off by the man-eater half an hour previously. With this information Nand Ram had come hot-foot to the Inspection Bungalow.

Ibbotson had had the Arab and the English mare saddled, and after we had eaten a good meal we set out, with Nand Ram to show us the way. There were no roads on the hill, only goat and cattle tracks, and as the big English mare found the hairpin bends on these tracks difficult to negotiate we sent the horses back and did the rest of the hot and steep climb on foot.

Arrived at the little isolated clearing in the forest, the two distracted women—-who appeared to be nursing the hope that the 'man of the house' might still be alive—showed us where Gawiya had been sitting near the door of the house when the leopard had seized him. The leopard had caught the unfortunate man by the throat, thus preventing him from making any sound, and after dragging him for a hundred yards had killed him. Then he had carried him for four hundred yards to a little hollow surrounded by dense brushwood. The wailing of the women and the .' shouting of Nand Ram had evidently disturbed the leopard at his meal, for he had only eaten the throat and jaw, and a small portion of one shoulder and thigh.

There were no trees within sight of the kill on which we could sit, so we poisoned the kill with cyanide at the three places where the leopard had eaten, and as it was now getting towards evening we took up position on a hill several hundred yards away, from where we could overlook the hollow in which the kill was lying. The leopard was undoubtedly in the dense brushwood, but though we lay in our concealed position and watched for two hours, we saw nothing of him. At dusk we lit the lantern we had provided ourselves with, and went back to the bungalow.

We were up very early next morning, and it was just getting light when we again sat down on the hill overlooking the hollow. We saw and heard nothing, and when the sun had been up an hour, we went to the kill; the leopard had not touched the three places where we had buried the poison, but had eaten the other shoulder and leg, and had then carried the body away for a short distance and hidden it under some bushes.

Again there were no trees overlooking the kill on which we could sit, and after a prolonged discussion we eventually decided that while Ibbotson went down the hill for a mile to a village where there was a big mango-tree, in which he could make himself a *machan* and spend the night, I would sit about four hundred yards from the kill, over a village path on which the previous day we had seen the pugmarks of the man-eater.

The tree I selected to sit in was a rhododendron which many years previously had been cut about fifteen feet above ground. Stout branches had grown out from the cut, and sitting on the old stump surrounded by the branches I had a perfect seat and perfect concealment.

Facing me was a steep well-wooded hill with a dense undergrowth of bracken and dwarf bamboo. Running across the face of the hill east and west was a well-used footpath; the rhododendron tree was growing about ten feet below this footpath.

From my seat in the tree I had an uninterrupted view of a length of about ten yards of the path, which to my left crossed a ravine and carried on at the same level on the far side, and to my right, and some three hundred yards farther on, passed a little below the bushes where the kill was lying. There was no water in the ravine where the path crossed it, but thirty yards lower down and immediately below, and three or four yards from, the root of my tree, there were several small pools—the start of a little spting which lower down became a stream providing drinking water to the villagers and irrigation for their crops.

The ten yards of path of which I had an uninterrupted view was joined at right-angles by a path coming down the hill from the house three hundred yards above me where Gawiya had been killed. Thirty yards up this path there was a bend, and from this point a small depression ran down to the lower path—the points where the depression started on the upper path and ended on the lower were not in my view.

There was no need for a torch, for it was a brilliant moonlit night, and if the leopard came along the level path or down the path from the house—as its pugmarks showed it had done the previous day—I should get an easy shot at a range of from twenty to forty feet.

I had gone down the hill a short distance with Ibbotson, and then a little before sunset had taken up my position on the tree. A few minutes later three *kalege* pheasants—a cock and two hens—came down the hill, and after drinking at the spring went back the way they had come. On both occasions they had passed under my tree, and that they had not seen me was proof that my hide was a good one.

The early part of the night was silent, but at eight o'clock a *kakar* started barking in the direction of the kill. The leopard had arrived, and I was convinced he had not gone to the kill along either of the paths I was watching. After barking for a few minutes the *kakar* stopped, and thereafter the night was again silent up to ten o'clock, when the *kakar* again barked. The leopard had been at the kill for two hours—sufficient time for him to have had a good meal, and for him to have poisoned himself several times over. And there was a good chance of his having done so, for on this second night the kill had been very effectively poisoned, the cyanide having been buried deep in the victim's flesh.

Without closing an eye I sat watching the hill in front of me, where the moonlight was so brilliant that I could clearly see every blade of grass, and at 2 a.m. I heard the leopard coming down the path from the direction of the house. I had scattered dry leaves on this path, and also on the lower path, with the object of getting some warning of the leopard's approach, and that he was now walking carelessly over these leaves, and not making any attempt at silence, filled me with hope—though I expected within the next few seconds to put a bullet into him—that all was not well with him.

At the bend in the path the leopard made a short pause, and then leaving the path entered the little depression and followed it down to the lower path, reaching which he again paused.

I had sat without movement for hours with my hands on the rifle lying across my knees, and as I was convinced that he would come along the path, I decided to let him pass in front of me, and when there was no longer any danger of his seeing the movement raise the rifle to my shoulder, and hit him where I wanted to. For seconds I watched the path, expecting to see his head appear from behind the screen of branches, and then, when tension was becoming unbearable, I heard him jump down off the path and come diagonally across the hill towards my tree. For a moment I thought he had in some mysterious way become aware of my presence on the tree and, not liking the flavour of his last kill, was intent on securing another human victim. His object, however, in leaving the path was not to try to get at me but to take a short cut down to the spring, for he passed the foot of the tree without a pause, and next second I heard him eagerly and noisily lapping water.

From the leopard's behaviour on the hill, and from the way he was now drinking, I was convinced he had poisoned himself, but not having had any previous experience of the effect of cyanide, I did not know how long the poison would take to act. For ten minutes after the leopard had stopped drinking, and just as I was beginning to hope that he had died at the spring, I heard him going up the hill on the far side of the ravine, all sound ceasing when he regained the path which carried on round the shoulder of the hill.

At no time, either when the leopard was coming down the path, coming down the depression, coming across the hill to the foot of my tree, when drinking, or going up the hill on the far side of the ravine, had I seen him, for either by accident or intent he had kept under cover to which not a glint of moonlight had penetrated. There was now no hope of my getting a shot, but this was not of much account if the poison was as potent as the doctor in Naini Tal had claimed that it was.

I sat on for the rest of the night, watching the path and listening for sounds. At daylight Ibbotson returned, and while we brewed ourselves a very welcome cup of tea I told him of the night's happenings.

On visiting the kill we found that the leopard had eaten the leg from which he had taken a small portion two nights previously, and in which we had buried a full dose of poison, and that he had in addition eaten two other doses of poison, one from the left shoulder and the other from the back.

It was now necessary to make a search for the leopard, and for this purpose the *patwari*, who had returned with Ibbotson, set off to collect men. At about midday the *patwari* returned with two hundred men, and with these we made a line and beat the whole side of the hill in the direction in which the leopard had gone.

Half a mile from where the leopard had quenched his thirst, and in the direct line in which I had heard him going away, there were some big rocks at the foot of which there was a cave extending far into the hill, with an opening large enough to admit a leopard. Near the mouth of this cave the leopard had scratched up the ground, and rid himself of his victim's toes—which he had swallowed whole.

Willing hands brought loose stones from the hillside, and when we left the cave we had sealed it beyond all possibility of any leopard that might be lurking in it escaping.

Next morning I returned with a roll of one-inch wire-netting and a number of iron tent-pegs, and, after removing the stones, very effectively wired up the mouth of the cave. Thereafter for the following ten days I visited the cave morning and evening, and as during this period no news of the man-eater came in from any village on the left bank of the Alaknanda, my hopes each day grew stronger that on my next visit I would surely get some indication that the leopard had died in the cave.

On the tenth morning, when I returned from my visit to the cave— where I had found the netting undisturbed—Ibbotson greeted me with the news that a woman had been killed the previous night in a village five miles away, and about a mile above the Rudraprayag-Badrinath pilgrim road.

Quite evidently cyanide was not the right poison for an animal that had the reputation of thriving on, and being stimulated by, arsenic and strychnine. That the leopard had eaten the cyanide there could be no doubt whatever, nor was there any doubt that he had entered the cave, for his hairs were adhering to the rock where his back had come in contact with it when entering the cave.

An overdose might account for the poison not having had the desired effect and a second opening somewhere farther up the hill might account for his escape from the cave. Even so, it was no longer any matter of surprise to me—who had only been acquainted with the leopard for a few short months—that the people of Garhwal, who had lived in close and intimate association with him for eight long years, should credit him— animal or spirit—with supernatural powers, and that they should cling to the belief that nothing but fire would rid them of this evil spirit.

TOUCH AND GO

News that is of importance to every individual travels fast, and during the past ten days everyone in Garhwal had heard of the poisoning of the man-eater, and of our hope that we had sealed it up in a cave. It was-natural therefore for risks to have been taken, and quite evidently the leopard, having recovered from the effects of the poison and found a way out of the cave, had found the first person who was taking a risk.

We had the day before us, for I had returned early from my visit to the cave, and after breakfast, mounted on Ibbotson's surefooted horses and carrying our rifles, we set out for the village where the woman was reported to have been killed.

After a fast ride up the pilgrim road we took a track that went diagonally across the hill, and a mile along this track, where the path from the village joined it, there were signs of a struggle and a big pool of blood.

The Headman, and relatives of the victim, were waiting for us at the village, and they showed us where the leopard had seized the woman as she was in the act of closing the door of her house behind her. From this point the leopard had dragged the woman along on her back for a hundred yards to the junction of the tracks, where he had released his hold, and after a violent struggle had killed her. The people in the village had heard the woman's screams as she was being dragged along the ground and as she was struggling for her life with the leopard, but had been too frightened to render any help.

When the woman was dead, the leopard had picked her up and carried her over some waste land, across an open ravine a hundred yards wide, and up the hill on the far side for another two hundred yards. There were no drag marks, but the blood trail was easy to follow, and it led us to a flat bit of ground, four feet wide and twenty feet long. On the upper side of this narrow strip of ground there was a perpendicular bank eight feet high with a stunted medlar-tree growing on it, and on the lower side of the narrow strip the hill fell steeply away, and growing on it was a wild rose-bush, which had reached up and smothered the medlar-tree. Lying huddled up between the steep bank and the rose-bush, with her head against the bank, with every vestige of clothing stripped from her, and with her naked body flecked with white rose-petals that had fallen from above was the kill—was an old grey-haired lady, seventy years of age.

Fof this pitiful kill the leopard would have to pay with his life, and after a short council of war, Ibbotson, leading the spare horse, returned to Rudraprayag for the things we needed, while I set off with my rifle to see whether it was possible to make contact with the man-eater in daylight.

This part of the country was new to me, and the first thing to do was to reconnoitre the ground. I had already noted while at the village that the hill went steeply up from the ravine to a height of four to five thousand feet; that about two thousand feet of the top of the hill was clothed with dense oak and pine forest, below which was an open stretch of short grass about half a mile wide, and that below the grass was scrub jungle.

Keeping now to the edge of the grass and scrub jungle I went round the shoulder of the hill, and found in front of me a wide depression, extending for half a mile down to the pilgrim road, and evidently caused in the days of long ago by a landslide. Beyond this depression, which was about a hundred yards wide at the upper end and about three hundred yards wide where it met the road, the ground was open. The ground in the depression was damp, and growing on this damp ground were a number of big trees, and under the tree a dense growth of scrub jungle. At the upper end of the depression was a cliff of overhanging rock, varying in height from twenty to forty feet, and about a hundred yards long; halfway along the cliff was a deep cleft a few feet wide, down which a tiny stream was trickling. Above the rocks was a narrow belt of scrub jungle, and above that again, open grassland.

I had reconnoitred the ground with care, for I did not want the leopard—which I was convinced was lying up in the depression—to be aware of my presence before it suited me. It was now necessary to find approximately where the leopard was most likely to be lying up, and to gain this information I went back to the kill.

We had been told in the village that it had got light shortly after the woman had been killed, and as it must have taken the leopard some little time to effect the kill, carry his victim four hundred yards, and eat a portion of it, it was reasonable to assume that he had left the spot where he had hidden the kill when day was fully established.

The hill on which the kill was lying was in full view of the village, in which at this hour there must had been considerable movement; the leopard therefore on leaving the kill would very naturally have kept to cover as far as was possible, and working on this assumption, and also because the ground was too hard to show pugmarks, I set out to follow him along the line I assumed he had taken.

When I'had covered half a mile and was out of view of the village and was approaching the depression, I was gratified to find that I had followed on the leopard's tracks foot by foot, for in the lee of a bush where there was some loose earth, I found where he had been lying for several hours. His pugmarks when leaving this spot showed that he had entered the depression about fifty yards below the cliff of rock.

For half an hour I lay where the leopard had lain, watching the small area'of tree and scrub jungle in front of me in the hope that the leopard would make some slight movement and give away his position.

After I had been watching for a few minutes a movement among the dead leaves attracted my attention, and presently two scimitar babblers came into view industriously turning over the leaves, looking for grubs. Where carnivores are concerned, these birds are among the most reliable informants in the jungle, and I hoped later to make use of this pair to help in locating the leopard.

No movement had been visible and no sound had come to indicate that the leopard was in the depression; but that he was there I was still convinced, and having failed to get a shot in one way I decided to try another way.

Without coming out into the open, there were two natural lines of retreat for the leopard, one down the hill towards the pilgrim road, and the other up the hill. To move him down the hill would not profit me, but if I moved him up the hill he would for a certainty go up the cleft in the rock cliff to gain the shelter of the bushes above the cliff, and while he was doing so, there was a reasonable chance of my getting a shot.

Entering the depression a little below where I thought the leopard was, I started to zigzag very slowly across it, gaining a few feet in height at each turn. There was as yet no need for me to keep an eye on the cleft, for the babblers were on the ground a few feet below it, and they would let me know when the leopard was on the move. I had gained about forty yards in height in my movements forward and backwards across the depression and was about ten yards from, and a little to the left of the cleft, when the babblers rose in alarm and, flying into a small oak tree and hopping about excitedly on the branches, started to give their clear and ringing alarm call, which can in the hills be heard for a distance of half a mile. Holding the rifle ready to take a snap shot, I stood perfectly still for a minute, and then started slowly moving forward.

The ground here was wet and slippery and, with my eyes fixed on the cleft, I had only taken two steps when my rubber-soled shoes slipped on ,' the wet surface; and while I was endeavouring to regain my balance, the leopard sprang up the cleft, and in the bushes above put up a covey of *kalege* pheasants, which came sailing down over my head.

My second attempt had failed, and though it would have been quite easy for me to have moved the leopard back to where he had started from, it would have been of no use for me to do so, for, from above, the cleft in the rock was not visible until one was right up to it, and long before I gained the position the leopard would have been far down the depression.

Ibbotson and I had arranged to meet in the open ravine at 2 p.m., and a little before that hour he returned from Rudraprayag, accompanied by several men carrying the things he had gone to fetch. These consisted of food, and drink—in the way of tea—our old friend the petromax lamp— which on this occasion I decided I would carry myself, if the necessity arose—two spare rifles and ammunition, my fishing-reel, a liberal supply of cyanide, and the gin-trap.

Sitting in the ravine by a clear stream of water, we had our lunch and brewed ourselves cups of tea, and then went over to the kill.

I will give a description of the position of the kill, to enable you to follow our movements and the subsequent happenings.

The kill was lying about five feet from the near or ravine end of the flat strip of ground, which was four feet wide and about twenty feet long. The upper side of this strip of ground was protected by a high bank, and the lower side by a steep drop and a spreading rose-bush. The stunted medlar tree on the bank was too small to allow a *machan* being made in it, so we decided to depend entirely on a gun-trap, poison, and the gin-trap; having come to this decision we set about our preparations.

First we poisoned the kill, of which the leopard had—for want of time—only eaten a small portion; hoping that on this occasion he would only consume sufficient to poison himself effectively, '[hen, while I bent over the kill in the position we anticipated the leopard would assume when eating, Ibbotson sighted and securely lashed his .256 Mannlicher— which had a hair trigger—and my .450 high-velocity rifle to two saplings, fifteen yards on our approach side of the kill.

There were no insuperable obstacles to the leopard getting at the kill from any side he might wish to, but his most natural line of approach from where I had left him was along the fifteen feet or so of flat ground, and on this strip of flat ground we proceeded to bury the huge gin-trap, first removing from the ground every dead leaf, bit of stick, and blade of grass that were lying on it.

After we had dug a hole sufficiently long, wide, and deep—removing the displaced earth to a distance—we put the gin-trap in it, and when the powerful springs that closed the jaws had been depressed, and the plate that constituted the trigger adjusted as delicately as we dared set it, we covered the whole trap with a layer of green leaves, over which we sprinkled earth, and blades of grass in the position we had found them. So t'arefully had the trap been set in the ground that we who had set it found it difficult to determine its exact position.

My fishing-reel was now produced and one end of the dressed silk line was tied to the trigger of one rifle, looped round the butt-end, and taken to within ten feet of the kill, from where it was taken back, looped round the butt-end of the second rifle, and tied to the trigger. The line was then cut—much to my regret, for it was a new and very good line—and after the end had been tied round the woman's waist, the line was passed through the loop, the lines to the triggers pulled taut, and a secure knot was tied. The line was then cut for the second time.

As we cast a final look over our handiwork—which appeared to us very good—it struck us that if the leopard was to wander round and approach the kill from our side, and not from the side we expected him to come, he might avoid both the guns and the gin-trap, and to prevent his doing so we sent to the village for a crowbar, while we cut five thornbushes from some little distance away. With the crowbar we made five holes a foot deep, on our side of the flat strip of ground, and into these holes we planted the bushes, stamping the earth round them and making them almost as secure and quite as natural to look at as when they were growing on the hillside. We were now quite satisfied that no animal bigger than a rat could approach the kill and eat any portion of it without meeting death in one form or another, so throwing off the safety catches of the rifles, we returned to the village.

Fifty yards from the village, and close to where we had on our arrival found the pool of blood, there was a big wide-spreading mango tree. In this tree we made a *machan* from planks procured from the village, and on it we piled a lot of sweet-smelling rice straw, for it was our intention to spend the night on it, in anticipation of having to finish off the leopard if he was caught in the gin-trap.

Near sundown we took our position on the *machan*, which was long enough for us to lie on at length and wide enough for us to lie side by side. The distance from the *machan* to the kill across the ravine was two hundred yards, and the kill was on a higher level than the *machan* by about a hundred (eef.

Ibbotson feared that his aim with the telescopic sight fitted to his rifle would not be quite accurate, so while he took a pair of powerful field glasses from their case, I loaded my .275 rifle. Our plan was that while Ibbotson concentrated on the portion of the hill along which we expected the leopard to come, I would keep a general look-out all over the hill, and if we saw the leopard, I would risk taking a shot, even if the shot had to be taken at the extreme range to which my rifle was sighted, which was three hundred yards.

While Ibbotson dozed, I smoked and watched the shadows cast by the hills in the west slowly creep up the hill in front of us, and when the rays from the setting sun were gilding the crest of the hill red, Ibbotson awoke and picked up his field glasses, and I picked up my rifle, for the time had now come when we could expect the leopard to make his appearance. There was still some forty five-minutes of daylight left, and during the time we intently scanned—I with a pair of eyes that few are blessed with, and Ibbotson with his field glasses—every foot of the considerable expanse of hill visible from our *machan*, without seeing the movement of a bird or animal.

When there was no longer sufficient light to shoot by, I put down my rifle, and a little later Ibbotson returned his field glasses to their case. One chance of killing the leopard had gone, but there were still three chances left, so we were not unduly depressed.

Shortly after dark it came on to rain, and I whispered to Ibbotson that I feared it would prove our undoing, for if the additional weight of rainwater on the delicately set gin-trap did not set it off, the contracting of the fishing-line due to getting wet, no matter how slight it might be, would to a certainty fire off his hair-trigger rifle. Some time later, and while it was still raining, Ibbotson asked me what time it was. I had a luminous wrist-watch, and I had just told him it was a quarter to eight when a succession of savage and angry roars came from the direction of the kill—the leopard, the much-famed man-eating leopard of Rudraprayag, was at long last in the gin-trap.

Ibbotson took a flying leap from the *machan* while I swung down from a branch, and that neither of us broke limbs in the descent can only be attributed to luck. The petromax lamp hidden in a nearby yam field was found, and while Ibbotson proceeded to light it, I gave expression to my fears and doubts, and admit I deserved Ibbotson's rejoinder, 'You are a rotten pessimist. First you think a few drops of rain are going to spring the trap ^tid fire off my rifle, and now you think because the leopard is not making a noise that it has got out of the trap.' That was just what I was thinking, and fearing, for on that other occasion when we had trapped a leopard it had roared and growled continuously, whereas this one, after that one expression of rage which had brought us tumbling out of the *machan*, had been ominously silent.

Ibbotson is an expert with all makes of lamps and in a very short time he had the petromax lit and pumped up, and throwing our doubts to the winds—for even Ibbotson was by now beginning to suspect the silence— we set off over the rough ground as hard as we could go, circling wide to avoid the fishing-lines and a possible angry leopard, and approached the loll from above. When we got to the high bank and looked down we saw the hole in the ground, but no gin-trap. Just as our hopes were bounding up, the brilliant light of the petromax revealed the trap; with its jaws closed and empty, ten yards down the hillside. The loll was no longer lying with its head against the bank, and a glance revealed that a considerable portion of it had been eaten.

Our thoughts were too bitter to give expression to as we went back to the mango tree and climbed into the *machan*. There was no longer any need for us to keep awake, so heaping some of the straw over ourselves, for we had no bedding and the night was cold, we went to sleep.

At the first streak of dawn a fire was built near the mango tree and water heated, and after we had drunk several cups of tea and warmed ourselves at the fire, we set off for the kill, accompanied by the *patwari* and several of Ibbotsons and my men, together with a number of men from the village.

I mention the fact that there were two of us, and that we had the *patwari* and a number of men with us, for had I been alone I would have hesitated to relate what I am now going to tell you.

Fiend or animal, had the slayer of the old woman been present and watched our overnight preparations it would even then have been difficult to understand how it had, on a dark and rainy night, avoided capture of death in one form or another. The rain, though light, had been sufficient to soften the ground, and we were able to reconstruct and to follow his every movement of the previous night.

The leopard had come from the direction from which we had expected him to come, and on arrival at the flat strip of ground, had skirted round and below it, and had then approached the kill from the side where we had firmly planted the thornbushes. Three of these bushes he had pulled up, making a sufficiently wide gap to go through, and then, getting hold of the kill, he had drawn it a foot or so towards the rifles, thus slackening off the fishing-lines. Having done this he had started to eat, avoiding while doing so contact with the fishing-line that was tied round the woman's body. We had not thought it necessary to poison either the head or the neck. These he had eaten first, and then—very carefully—he had eaten all that portion of the body between the many doses of poison we had inserted in different places.

After satisfying his hunger the leopard left the kill with the intention of seeking shelter from the rain and, while he was doing so, what I feared would happen actually happened. The weight of rainwater on the very finely set trap had depressed the plate that constituted the trigger, and released the springs just as the leopard was stepping over the trap, and the great jaws had met on either side of the stifle, or knee-joint, of his hind leg. And here was the greatest tragedy of all, for when bringing the trap up from Rudraprayag the men carrying it had let it fall, and one of the three- inch-long teeth had been broken off, and the stifle of the leopard's left hind leg had been caught by the jaws exactly where this missing tooth formed a gap in the otherwise perfectly fitting set of teeth. But for this missing tooth the leopard would have been fixed to the trap without any possibility of getting free, for the grip on his leg had been sufficiently good for him to lift the eighty-pound trap out of the hole in which we had buried it, and carry it ten yards down the hillside. And now, instead of the leopard, the jaws of the trap only held a tuft of hair and a small piece of skin, which we later—much later—had the great satisfaction of fitting back into position.

However unbelievable the actions of the leopard may appear to have been, they were in fact just what one would have expected from an animal that had been a man-eater for eight years. Avoiding the open ground, and approaching the kill under cover; removing the thorn obstruction we had erected across the blood trail he had left that morning; pulling the kill towards him into a convenient position for his meal, and rejecting those portions of the kill that we had poisoned—cyanide, of which he now had experience, has a very strong smell—were all quite normal and natural actions.

The explanation I have given for the springing of the trap is, I am convinced, correct. It was just a coincidence that the leopard happened to be directly over the trap the very moment that the additional weight of water set it off.

Having dismantled the gin-trap, and waited until the relatives had removed .what remained of the old woman for cremation, we set out to walk back to Rudraprayag, leaving our men to follow us. Some time during the night the leopard had come to the mango tree, for we found his pugmarks near the tree where the pool of blood—now washed away by the rain—had been, and we followed these pugmarks down the track to the pilgrim road and four miles along the road to the gate of the Inspection Bungalow where, after scratching up the ground at the base of one of the pillars of the gate, he had gone on down the road for another mile to where my old friend the packman was camped, one of whose goats he had wantonly killed.

I need not tell those of you who have carried a sporting rifle in any part of the world that all these many repeated failures and disappointments, so far from discouraging me, only strengthened my determination to carry on until that great day or night came when, having discarded poisons and traps, I would get an opportunity of using my rifle as rifles were intended to be used, to put a bullet truly and accurately into the man-eater's body.

A LESSON IN CAUTION

I have never agreed with those sportsmen who attribute all their failures in big-game hunting to their being Jonahs.

The thoughts of a sportsman, whether they be pessimistic or whether they be optimistic, sitting waiting for an animal, cannot in any conceivable way influence the actions of the animal he is endeavouring to shoot or, maybe, to photograph.

We are apt to forget that the hearing and sight of wild animals, and especially of those animals that depend exclusively on these senses not only for food but also for self-preservation, are on a plane far and away above that of civilized human beings, and that there is no justification for us to assume that because we cannot hear or see the movements of our prospective quarry, our quarry cannot hear or see our movements. A wrong estimation of the intelligence of animals, and the inability to sit without making any sound or movement for the required length of time, is the cause of all failures when sitting up for animals. As an example of the acute sense of hearing of carnivores, and the care it is necessary to exercise when contact with one of them is desired, I will relate one of my recent experiences.

On a day in March, when the carpet of dry leaves on the ground recorded the falling of every dead leaf and the movements of the smallest of the birds that feed on the ground, I located in some very heavy undergrowth the exact position of a tiger I had long wished to photograph, by moving a troop of *langurs* in the direction in which I suspected the tiger to be lying up. Seventy yards from the tiger there was an open glade, fifty yards long and thirty yards wide. On the edge of the glade, away from the tiger, there was a big tree overgrown with creepers that extended right up to the topmost branches; twenty feet from the ground the tree forked in two. I knew that the tiger would cross the glade in the late afternoon, for the glade lay directly between him and his sambhar kill which I had found early that morning. There was no suitable cover near the kill for the tiger to lie up in during the day, so he had gone to the heavy undergrowth where the *langurs* had located him for me.

It is often necessary, when shooting or photographing tigers and leopards on foot, to know the exact position of one's quarry, whether it be a wounded animal that one desires to put out of its misery or an animal that one wants to photograph, and the best way of doing this is by enlisting the help of birds or animals. With patience, and with a knowledge of the habit of the bird or animal the sportsman desires to use, it is not difficult to get a particular bird or animal to go in the required direction. The birds most suitable for this purpose are red jungle-fowl, peafowl, and white-capped babblers, and of animals the most suitable are *kakar*s and *langurs*.

The tiger I am telling you about was unwounded and it would have been quite easy for me to go into the undergrowth and find him myself, but in doing so I should have disturbed him and defeated my own purposes, whereas by using the troop of *langurs* and knowing what their reactions would be on sighting the tiger—if he happened to be in the undergrowth—I was able to get the information I wanted without disturbing the tiger.

Very carefully I stalked the tree I have referred to, and avoiding contact with the creepers, the upper tendrils and leaves of which might have been visible from where the tiger was lying, I climbed to the fork, where I had a comfortable seat and perfect concealment. Getting out my 16-mm cine¬camera I made an opening in the screen of leaves in front of me just big enough to photograph through, and having accomplished all this without having made a sound, I sat still. My field of vision was confined to the glade and to the jungle immediately beyond it.

After I had been sitting for an hour, a pair of bronzewing doves rose out of the jungle and went skimming over the low brushwood, and a minute or two later, and a little closer to me, a small flight of upland pipits rose off the ground and, after daintily tripping along the branches of a leafless tree, rose above the tree-tops and went off. Neither of these two species of birds has any alarm call, but I knew from their behaviour that the tiger was afoot and that they had been disturbed by him. Minutes later I was slowly turning my eyes from left to right scanning every foot of ground visible to me, when my eyes came to rest on a small white object, possibly an inch or two square, immediately in front of me, and about ten feet from the edge of the glade. Focusing my eyes on this stationary object for a little while, I then continued to scan the bushes to the limit of my field of vision to the right, and then back again to the white object.

I was now convinced that this object had not been where it was for more than a minute or two before I had first caught sight of it, and that it could not be anything other than a white mark on the tiger's face. Quite evidently the tiger had heard me when I was approaching or climbing the tree, though I had done this in thin rubber shoes without making as far as I was aware any sound, and when the time had come for him to go to his kill he had stalked, for a distance of seventy yards over dry leaves, the spot he had pin-pointed as the source of some suspicious sound. After lying for half an hour without making any movement, he stood up, stretched himself, yawned, and, satisfied that he had nothing to fear, walked out into the glade. Here he stood, turning his head first to the right and then to the left, and then crossed the glade, passing right under my tree on his way to his kill.

When in my wanderings through the jungles I see the *machan* that have been put up for the purpose of shooting carnivores, and note the saplings that have been felled near by to make the platform, the branches that have been cut to give a clear view, and see the litter and debris left lying about, and consider the talking and noise that must have accompanied these operations, I am not surprised when I hear people say they have sat up hundreds of times for tigers and leopards without ever having seen one of these animals, and attribute their failures to their being Jonahs.

Our failure to bag the man-eater up to that date was not due to our having done anything we should not have done, or left undone anything we should have done. It could only be attributed to sheer bad luck. Bad luck that had prevented my receiving the electric light in time; that had given Ibbotson cramps in both legs; that had made the leopard eat an overdose of cyanide; and, finally, that had made the men drop the gin-trap and break the one tooth that mattered. So when Ibbotson returned to Pauri, after our failure to kill the leopard over the body of his seventy-year- old victim, I was full of hope, for I considered my chances of shooting the leopard as good as they were on the first day I arrived at Rudraprayag, and in fact better than they had then been, for I now knew the capabilities of the animal I had to deal with.

One thing was causing me a lot of uneasiness and much heart¬searching, and that was confining the man-eater to one bank of the river. However I looked at it, it did not appear to be right that the people on the left bank of the Alaknanda should be exposed to attacks by the leopard, while the people on the right bank were free from the risk of such attacks. Including the boy killed two days before our arrival, three people had recently lost their lives on the left bank, and others might meet with a like fate, and yet to open the two bridges and let the leopard cross over to the right bank would add an hundredfold to my difficulties, which were already considerable, and would not benefit Garhwal as a whole, for the lives'of the people on the right bank of the river were just as valuable as the lives of the people on the left bank; so, very reluctantly, I decided to keep the bridges closed. And here I should like to pay my tribute to the people—numbering many thousands—living on the left bank of the river who, knowing that the closing of the bridges was confining the activities of the dread man-eater to their area, never once, during the months f .closed the bridges, removed the barriers themselves, or asked me to do so.

Having decided to keep the bridges closed, I sent a man to warn the villagers of their danger, and myself carried the warning to as many villages as time and my ability to walk permitted of my doing. No one whom I talked with on the roads and in the villages ever expressed one word of resentment at the leopard having been confined to their area, and everywhere I went I was offered hospitality and speeded on my way with blessings, and I was greatly encouraged by the assurances from both men and women—who did not know but what they might be the man-eater's next victim—that it was no matter for regret that the leopard had not died yesterday, for surely it would die today or, maybe, tomorrow.

A WILD BOAR HUNT

The old packman had arrived at the thorn enclosure late the previous evening. He was packing salt and gur from the bazaar at Hardwar to the villages beyond Badrinath, and as his flock of sheep and goats was heavily laden and the last march had been a long one, he had arrived too late at the thorn enclosure to repair the weak places in it, with the result that several of the goats had strayed out of the enclosure and one of them the leopard had killed, close to the road, during the early hours of the morning. The barking of his dogs had awakened him, and when it got light, he saw his best goat—a beautiful steel-grey animal nearly as large as a Shetland pony—lying dead near the road, wantonly killed by the man-eater.

The behaviour of the man-eater during the previous night showed the extent to which the habits of a leopard change when it has become a man- eater and has lived in close association with human beings over a long period of years.

It was reasonable to assume that the man-eater had received a great shock, and a great fright, by being caught in the gin-trap; his having carried the heavy trap for ten yards and the angry way in which he had roared were in fact proof of this; and one would have expected him, the moment he got out of the trap, to have retired to some secluded spot as far removed from human habitation as possible, and to have remained there until he was again hungry, which he would not be for several days. But, so far from doing this, he had quite evidently remained in the vicinity of the kill, and after watching us climb into the *machan* and giving us time to go to sleep, had come to investigate; fortunately for us, Ibbotson had taken the precaution to protect the *machan* by putting wire-netting all round it, for it is not an unheard-of thing for man-eating leopards to kill people who are sitting up trying to shoot them. At the present time there is a man-eating leopard in the Central Provinces that has—at different times—killed and eaten four Indian sportsmen who were trying to shoot him; up to the time I last heard of this animal he had killed forty human beings, and owing to his habit of eating his would-be slayers, he was living a very peaceful and undisturbed life, varying his human diet with game and domestic animals.

After his visit to the mango tree, our man-eater went along the village path to its»junction with the track. Here, where we had found the pool of blood, he had turned to the right and gone down the track for a mile, and then along the pilgrim road for another four miles and into the most densely populated part of the area in which he was operating. On arrival at Rudraprayag, he had gone through the main street of the bazaar, and half a mile farther on had scratched up the ground at the gate of the Inspection Bungalow. The rain of the previous night had softened the clay surface of the road, and on the soft clay the pugmarks of the leopard showed up clearly, and from them it was possible to see that the leopard's encounter with the gin-trap had not resulted in injury to any of his limbs.

After breakfast I took up the tracks at the gate and followed them to the packman's camp. From a bend in the road, a hundred yards from the camp, the leopard had caught sight of the goats that had strayed from the enclosure, and crossing from the outer to the inner edge of the road and creeping along under shelter of the hill he had stalked the grazing animals and, after killing the steel-grey goat but without even troubling to drink its blood, had returned to the road.

In the thorn enclosure, guarding the dead goat and the neatly stacked pile of packs, were the packman's two sheep-dogs, tethered to stout pegs with short lengths of heavy chain. These big, black, and powerful dogs that are used by packmen throughout our hills are not accredited sheep¬dogs in the same sense that sheep-dogs in Great Britain and in Europe are. On the march the dogs keep close to heel, and their duties—which they perform very efficiently—start when camp is made. At night they guard the camp against wild animals—I have known two of them to kill a leopard—and during the day and while the packmen are away grazing the flock they guard the camp against all intruders. A case is on record of one of these dogs having killed a man who was attempting to remove a pack from the camp it had been left to guard.

I picked up the tracks of the leopard where he returned to the road after killing the goat, and followed them through Golabrai and for a mile farther on, to where a deep ravine crosses the road, up which he had gone. The distance the leopard had covered from the mango tree to the ravine was about eight miles. This long and seemingly aimless walk away from a kill was in itself a thing no ordinary leopard would under any circumstances have undertaken, nor would an ordinary leopard have killed a goat when he was not hungry.

A quarter of a mile beyond the ravine the old packman was sitting on a rock by the side of the road, spinning wool and watching his flock, which Vere grazing on the open hillside. When he had dropped his spinning-stick and wool into the capacious pocket in his blanket robe and accepted a cigarette, he asked if I had come past his camp. When I told him I had done so and that I had seen what the evil spirit had done, and added that it would be wise to sell his dogs to camelmen on his next visit to Hardwar, for it was quite evident that they were larking in courage, he nodded his head as one in agreement with what he heard. Then he said, '*Sahib*, even we old hands are apt at times to make mistakes, and suffer for them, even as I have this night suffered by losing my best goat. My dogs have the courage of tigers, and are the best dogs in all Garhwal, and it is an insult to them for you to say they are only fit to be sold to camelmen. My camp as you doubtless observed, is very close to the road, and I feared that if by chance anyone came along the road by night, my dogs might do him an injury, so I chained them up outside the thorn enclosure instead of leaving them loose, as is my wont. You have seen the result; but do not blame the dogs, *sahib*, for in their efforts to save my goat their collars have bitten deep into their necks, and made wounds that will take many days to heal.'

While we were talking, an animal appeared on the crest of the hill on the far side of the Ganges. From its colour and size, I at first thought it was a Himalayan bear, but when it started to come down the hill towards the river, I saw it was a big wild boar. The pig was followed by a pack of village pye dogs, who in turn were followed by a rabble of boys and men, all armed with sticks of varying size. Last of all came a man carrying a gun. As this man crested the hill he raised his piece and we saw a puff of smoke, and a little later heard the dull report of a muzzle-loading gun. The only living things within range of the gun were the boys and men, but as none of them dropped out of the race, the sportsman appeared to have missed them.

The pig had a long grassy slope before him, with an odd bush dotted here and there, and below the grass slope was some broken ground, and below that again a dense belt of brushwood which extended right down to the river.

On the rough broken ground the pig lost his lead, and pig and pye dogs disappeared into the brushwood together. Next minute all the dogs, with the exception of the big light-coloured animal that had been leading the pack, dashed back out of the brushwood. When the boys and men arrived they appeared to urge the dogs to re-enter the cover, but this—after apparently having recently seen what the pig could do with his tusks—they were unwilling to do. The man with the gun then arrived,,and was immediately surrounded by the boys and men.

To us sitting on our elevated grandstand with the river flowing between, the scene being enacted on the farther hill was a silent picture, for the noise of the water deadened sound and all we had heard was the dull report of the muzzle-loader.

The sportsman was apparently as reluctant to enter the cover as the dogs were, for presently he broke away from his companions and sat down oh a rock, as if to say, 'I have done my bit, now you do yours.' Confronted with this double dilemma—for the dogs, even after some of them had been beaten, stoutly refused to face the pig—first the boys and then the men started to throw stones into the brushwood.

While this was going on, we saw the pig emerge from the lower end of the brushwood on to a narrow strip of sand. With a few quick steps he came out into the open, stood perfectly still for a few seconds, took a few more steps, stopped again, and then with a little run plunged into the river. Pigs—the wild variety—are exceptionally good swimmers, and they do not cut their throats with their hooves while swimming, as is generally believed.

The current in the river was strong, but there is no bigger-hearted animal than our wild pig, and when I last saw the old boar he had been washed down the river a quarter of a mile, but was swimming strongly and was nearing our bank, which I have no doubt he reached safely.

'Was the pig within range of your rifle, *sahib*V asked the packman.

'Yes,' I replied, 'the pig was within range, but I have not brought a rifle to Garhwal to shoot pigs that are running for their lives, but to shoot what you think is an evil spirit, and what I know is a leopard.'

'Have it your own way,' he rejoined; 'and now, as you are going, and we may never meet again, take my blessings with you, and time will prove whether you or I am right.'

I regret I never saw the packman again, for he was a grand old man, as proud as Tucifer, and as happy as the day was long, when leopards were not killing his best goats and when the courage of his dogs was not being questioned.

VIGIL ON A PINE TREE

Ibbotson returned to Pauri next day, and the following morning, when I was visiting the villages on the hill to the east of Rudraprayag, I found the tracks of the man-eater on a path leading out of a village in which the previous night he had tried to break open the door of a house in which there was a child suffering from a bad cough. On following the tracks for a couple of miles they led me to the shoulder of the mountain where, some days previously, Ibbotson and I had sat up over the calling goat which the leopard had later killed.

It was still quite early, and as there was a chance of finding the leopard basking on one of the rocks in this considerable area of broken ground, I lay on a projecting rock that commanded an extensive view. It had rained the previous evening—thus enabling me to track the leopard—and washed the haze out of the atmosphere. Visibility was at its best and the view from the projecting rock was as good as could be seen in any part of the world where mountains rise to a height of twenty-three thousand feet. Immediately below me was the beautiful valley of the Alaknanda, with the river showing as a gleaming silver ribbon winding in and out of it. On the hill beyond the river, villages were dotted about, some with only a single thatched hut, and others with long rows of slate-roofed houses. These row buildings are in fact individual homesteads, built one against the other to save expense and to economize space, for the people are poor and every foot of workable land in Garhwal is needed for agriculture.

Beyond the hills were rugged rock cliffs, down which avalanches roar in winter and early spring, and beyond and above the cliffs were the eternal snows, showing up against the intense blue sky as clear as if cut out of white cardboard. No more beautiful or peaceful scene could be imagined, and yet when the sun, now shining on the back of my head, set on the far side of the snow mountains, terror—terror which it is not possible to imagine until experienced—-would grip, as it had done for eight long years, the area I was now overlooking.

I had been lying on the rock for an hour when two men came down the hill, on their way to the bazaar. They were from a village about a mile farther up the hill that I had visited the previous day, and they informed me that a little before sunrise they had heard a leopard calling in this direction. We discussed the possibilities of my getting a shot at the leopard over a goat, and as at that time I had no goats of my own, they offered to bring me one from their village and promised to meet me where we were standing, two hours before sunset.

When the men had gone I looked round for a place where I could sit. The only tree on the whole of this part of the mountain was a solitary pine. It was growing on the ridge close to the path down which the men had come, and from under it a second path took off and ran across the face of the mountain skirting the upper edge of the broken ground, where I had recently been looking for the leopard. The tree commanded an extensive view, but it could be difficult to climb, and would afford little cover. However, as it was the only tree in the area, I had no choice, so I decided I would try it.

The men were waiting for me with a goat when I returned at about 4 p.m., and when, in reply to their question where I intended sitting, I pointed to the pine, they started laughing. Without a rope ladder, they said, it would not be possible to climb the tree; and further, if I succeeded in climbing the tree without a ladder, and carried out my intention of remaining out all night, I should have no protection against the man- eater, to whom the tree would offer no obstacle. There were two white men in Garhwal—Ibbotson was one of them—who had collected birds' eggs when boys, and both of whom could climb the tree; and as there is no exact equivalent in Hindustani for 'waiting until you come to a bridge before crossing it', I let the second part of the men's objection go unanswered, contenting myself by pointing to my rifle.

The pine was not easy to climb, for there were no branches for twenty feet, but once having reached the lowest branch, the rest was easy. I had provided myself with a long length of cotton cord, and when the men had tied my rifle to one end of it, I drew it up and climbed to the top of the tree, where the pine-needles afforded most cover.

The men had assured me that the goat was a good caller, and after they tied it to an exposed root of the tree they set off for their village promising to return early next morning. The goat watched the men out of sight, and then started to nibble the short grass at the foot of the tree. The fact that it had not up to then called once did not worry me, for I felt sure that it would presently feel lonely and that it would then do its share of the business of the evening, and if it did it while it was still night, from my elevated position I should be able to kill the leopard long before it got anywhere near the goat.

When I climbed the tree the shadows cast by the snow mountains had reached the Alaknanda. Slowly these shadows crept up the hill and passed me, until,only the top of the mountain glowed with red light. As this glow faded, long streamers of light shot up from the snow mountains where the rays of the setting sun were caught and held on a bank of clouds as soft and as light as thistledown. Everyone who has eyes to see a sunset— and the number, as you might have observed, is regrettably few—thinks that the sunsets in his particular part of the world are the best ever. I am no exception, for I too think that there are no sunsets in all the world to "compare with ours, and a good second are the sunsets in northern Tanganyika, where some quality in the atmosphere makes snow-capped Kilimanjaro, and the clouds that are invariably above it, glow like molten gold in the rays of the setting sun. Our sunsets in the Himalayas are mostly red, pink, or gold. The one I was looking at the evening from my seat on the pine tree was rose pink, and the white shafts of light, starting as spear- points from valleys in the cardboard snows, shot through the pink clouds and, broadening, faded out in the sky overhead.

The goat, like many human beings, had no interest in sunsets, and after nibbling the grass within reach, scratched a shallow hole for itself, lay down, curled up, and went to sleep. Here was a dilemma. I had counted on the animal now placidly sleeping below me to call up the leopard, and not once since I had first seen it had it opened its mouth, except to nibble grass, and now, having made itself comfortable, it would probably sleep throughout the night. To have left the tree at that hour in an attempt to return to the bungalow would have added one more to the number who deliberately commit suicide, and as I had to be doing something to kill the man-eater, and as—in the absence of a kill—one place was as good as another, I decided to stay where I was, and try to call up the leopard myself.

If I were asked what had contributed most to my pleasure during all the years that I have spent in Indian jungles, I would unhesitatingly say that I had derived most pleasure from a knowledge of the language, and the habits, of the jungle folk. There is no universal language in the jungles; each species has its own language, and though the vocabulary of some is limited, as in the case of porcupines and vultures, the language of each species is understood by all the jungle folk. The vocal chords of human beings are more adaptable than the vocal chords of any of the jungle folk, with the one exception of the crested wire-tailed drongo, and for this reason it is possible for human beings to hold commune with quite a big range of birds and animals. The ability to speak the language of the jungle folk, apapt from adding hundredfold to one's pleasure in the jungle, can, if so desired, be put to great use. One example will suffice.

Lionel Fortescue—up till recently a housemaster at Eton—and I were on a photographing and fishing tour in the Himalayas shortly after 1918, and we arrived one evening at a Forest Bungalow at the foot of a great mountain, on the far side of which was our objective, the Vale of Kashmir. We had been marching over hard ground for many days, and as the men carrying our luggage needed a rest, we decided to halt for a day at the bungalow. Next day, while Fortescue wrote up his notes, I set out to explore the mountain and try for a Kashmir stag. I had been informed by friends who had shot in Kashmir that it was not possible to shoot one of these stags without the help of an experienced *shikari*, and this was confirmed by the *chowkidar* in charge of the Forest Bungalow. With the whole day before me I set out alone, after breakfast, without having the least idea at what elevation the red deer lived, or the kind of ground on which they were likely to be found. The mountain, over which there is a pass into Kashmir, is about twelve thousand feet high, and after I had climbed to a height of eight thousand a storm came on.

From the colour of the clouds I knew I was in for a hailstorm, so I selected with care a tree under which to shelter. I have seen both human beings and animals killed by hail, and by the lightning that invariably accompanies hailstorms, so rejecting the big fir trees with tapering tops I selected a small tree with a rounded top and dense foliage, and collecting a supply of dead wood and fir-cones, I built a fire, and for the hour that the thunder roared overhead and the hail lashed down, I sat at the foot of my tree safe and warm.

The moment the hail stopped the sun came out, and from the shelter of the tree I stepped into fairyland, for the hail that carpeted the ground gave off a million points of light to which every glistening leaf and blade of grass added its quota. Continuing up for another two or three thousand feet, I came on an outcrop of rock, at the foot of which was a bed of blue mountain poppies. The stalks of many of these, the most beautiful of all wild flowers in the Himalayas, were broken, even so these sky-blue flowers standing in a bed of spotless white were a never-to-be-forgotten sight.

The rocks were too slippery to climb, and there appeared to be no object in going to the top of the hill, so keeping to the con tours I went to the left, and after half a mile through a forest of giant fir trees I came to a grassy slope which, starting from the top of the hill, extended several thousand feet down into the forest. As I came through the trees towards this grassy slope I saw on the far side of it an animal standing on a little knoll, with its tail towards me. From illustrations seen in game books I knew the animal was a red Kashmir deer, and when it raised its head, I saw it was a hind.

On my side of the grassy slope, and about thirty yards from the edge of the forest, there was a big isolated rock some four feet high; the distance between this rock and the knoll was about forty yards. Moving only when the deer was cropping the grass, and remaining still each time she raised her head, I crept up to the shelter of the rock. The hind was quite obviously a sentinel, and from the way she looked to her right each time she raised her head, I knew she had companions, and the exact direction in which these companions were. To approach any nearer over the grass without being seen was not possible. To re-enter the forest and work down from above would not have been difficult but would have defeated my purpose, for the wind was blowing down the hill. There remained the alternative of re-entering the forest and skirting round the lower end of the grass slope, but this would take time and entail a stiff climb. I therefore finally decided to remain where I was and see if these deer—which I was seeing for the first time—would react in the same way as chital and sambhar do to the call of a leopard, of which I knew there was at least one on the mountain, for I had seen its scratch-marks earlier in the day. With only one eye showing, I waited until the hind was cropping the grass, and then gave the call of a leopard.

At the first sound of my voice the hind swung round and, facing me, started to strike the ground with her forefeet. This was a warning to her companions to be on the alert, but those companions whom I wanted to see would not move until the hind called, and this she would not do until she saw the leopard. I was wearing a brown tweed coat, and projecting a few inches of my left shoulder beyond the rock I moved it up and down. The movement was immediately detected by the hind, who, taking a few quick steps forward, started to call; the danger she had warned her companions of was in sight, and it was now safe for them to join her. The first to come was a yearling, which, stepping daintily over the hail-covered ground, ranged itself alongside the hind; the yearling was followed by three stags, who in turn were followed by an old hind. The entire herd, numbering six in all, were now in full view at a range of thirty-five yards. The hind was still calling, while the others, with ears alternately held rigid or feeling forward and backward for sound and wind direction, were standing perfectly still and gazing into the forest behind me. My seat on tha'melting hail was uncomfortable and wet, and to remain inactive longer would possibly result in a cold. I had seen a representative herd of the much-famed Kashmir deer, and I had heard a hind call, but there was one thing more that I wanted. That was, to hear a stag call; so I again projected a few inches of my shoulder beyond the rock, and had the satisfaction of hearing the stags, the hinds, and the yearling calling in different pitched keys.

My pass permitted me to shoot one stag, and for all I knew one of the stags might have carried a record head, but though I had set out that morning to look for a stag, and procure meat for the camp, I now realized that I was in no urgent need of a trophy. In any case the stag's meat would probably be tough so, instead of using the rifle, I stood up, and six of the most surprised deer in Kashmir vanished out of sight, and a moment later I heard them crashing through the undergrowth on the far side of the knoll.

It was now time for me to retrace my steps to the bungalow, and I decided to go down the grassy slope and work through the lighter forest at the foot of the mountain. The slope was at an angle that lent itself to an easy lope, provided care was taken to see that every step was correctly placed. I was running in the middle of the hundred-yard open ground and had gone about six hundred yards when I caught sight of a white object, standing on a rock at the edge of the forest on the left-hand side of the slope, and about three hundred yards below me. A hurried glance convinced me that the white object was a goat, that had probably been lost in the forest. We had been without meat for a fortnight and I had promised Fortescue that I would bring something back with me, and there was my opportunity. The goat had seen me, and if I could disarm suspicion would possibly let me pass close enough to catch it by the legs; so as I loped along I edged to the left, keeping the animal in sight out of the corner of my eyes. Provided the animal stayed where it was, no better place on all the mountain could have been found on which to catch it, for the flat rock, at the very edge of which it was standing, jutted out into the slope, and was about five feet high. Without looking directly at it, and keeping up a steady pace, I ran past the rock and, as I did so, made a sweep with my left hand for its forelegs. With a sneeze of alarm the animal reared up, avoiding my grasp, and when I pulled up clear of the rock and turned round, I saw to my amazement that the animal I had mistaken for a white goat was an albino musk-deer. With only some ten feet between us the game little animal was standing its ground and sneezing defiance at me. Turning away I walked down the hill for fifty yards, and when I looked back, the deer was still standing on the rock, possibly congratulating itself on having frightened me away. When some weeks later I related the occurrence to the Game Warden of Kashmir he expressed great regret at my not having shot the deer, and was very anxious to know the exact locality in which I had seen it, but as my memory for places, and my description of localities, is regrettably faulty, I do not think that particular albino musk-deer is gracing any museum.

() () ()

Male leopards are very resentful of intrusion of others of their kind in the area they consider to be their own. True, the man-eater's territory extended over an area of five hundred square miles in which there were possibly many other male leopards; still, he had been in this particular area for several weeks, and might very reasonably consider it his own. And again, the mating season was only just over, and the leopard might mistake my call for the call of a female in search of a mate, so waiting until it was quite dark I called and, to my surprise and delight, was immediately answered by a leopard some four hundred yards below and a little to the right.

The ground between us was strewn with great rocks and overgrown with matted thornbushes, and I knew the leopard would not come in a straight line towards me, and that he would probably skirt round the broken ground and come up a subsidiary ridge to the one my tree was on; this I found, when next he called, that he was doing. Five minutes later I located his call as coming from the path that, starting from my tree, ran across the face of the hill, about two hundred yards away. This call I answered, to give the leopard direction. Three, or it may have been four, minutes later, he called again from a distance of a hundred yards.

It was a dark night and I had an electric torch lashed to the side of my rifle, and my thumb on the push button. From the root of the tree the path ran in a straight line for fifty yards, to where there was a sharp bend in it. It would not be possible for me to know when or where to direct the beam of the torch on this part of the path, so I should have to wait until the leopard was on the goat.

Just beyond the bend, and only sixty yards away, the leopard again called, and was answered by another leopard far up the mountain-side. A complication as unexpected as it was unfortunate, for my leopard was too close now for me to call, and as he had last heard me from a distance of two hundred yards he would naturally assume that the coy female had /removed herself farther up the hill and was calling to him to join her there. There was, however, just a possibility of his continuing along the path to its junction with the path coming down the hill, in which case he would be sure to kill the goat, even if he had no use for it. But the goat's luck was in, and mine out, for the leopard cut across the angle formed by the two paths, and the next time he called he was a hundred yards farther from me, and a hundred yards nearer his prospective coaxing mate. The calling of the two leopards drew nearer and nearer together, and finally stopped. After a long period of silence the caterwauling of these two giant cats came floating down to me from where I judged the grassland ended and the dense forest began.

The leopard's luck was unfortunately in, in more ways than one, not least of all because it was dark, for leopards when courting are very easy to shoot. The same can be said of tigers, but the sportsman who goes on foot to look for courting tigers should be quite sure that he wants to see them, for a tigress—never a tiger—is very sensitive at these times, and quite understandably so, for males of the cat tribe are rough in their courting, and do not know how-sharp their claws are.

The leopard had not died, nor would he die that night, but maybe he would die the next day, or the day after, for his sands were running out; and so for a long moment I thought were mine, for without any warning a sudden blast of wind struck the tree, and my heels and my head changed their relative position with the land of Garhwal. For seconds I thought it impossible for the tree to regain its upright position, or for me to retain contact with it. When the pressure eased, the tree and I got back to where we were before the wind struck us, and fearing that worse might follow, I hurriedly tied the rifle to a branch, to have the use of both hands. The pine had possibly withstood many wind-storms equally bad, if not worse, but never with a human being on it to add weight and increase wind-pressure. When the rifle was safe, I climbed out on to one branch after another, and broke off all the tassels of pine-needles that I could reach. It may only have been my imagination, but after I had lightened the tree it did not appear to heel over as dangerously as it had at first done. Fortunately the pine was comparatively young and supple, and its roots firm set, for it was tossed about like a blade of grass for an hour and then, as suddenly as it had started, the wind died down. There was no possibility of the leopard returning, so, after I had smoked a cigarette, I followed the goat into the land of dreams.

As the sun was rising a cooee brought me back to within fifty feet of earth, and under the tree were my two companions of the previous evening, reinforced by two youths from their village. When they saw that I was awake they asked whether I had heard the leopards during the night, and what had happened to the tree, and were hugely amused when I told them I had had a friendly conversation with the leopards, and that having nothing else to do I had amused myself by breaking the branches of the tree. I then asked them if by chance they had noticed that there had been some, little wind during the night, on which one of the youths answered, 'A little wind, *sahib*! Such a big wind has never been known, and it has blown away my hut!' To which his companion rejoined, 'That is no matter for regret, *sahib*, for Sher Singh has long been threatening to rebuild his hut, and the wind has saved him the trouble of dismantling the old one.'

MY NIGHT OF TERROR

For several days after my experience on the pine tree I lost touch with the man-eater. He did not return to the broken ground and I found no trace of him, or of the female who had saved his life, in the miles of forest. I searched on the high ground above the cultivated land. In these forests I was more at home, and if the leopards had been anywhere in them I should have been able to find them, for there were birds and animals in the forest that would have helped me.

The female, being restless, was quite evidently straying far from her home when she heard me call from the top of the pine tree, and on being joined by the male had gone back to her own area, accompanied by the mate I had helped her to find. The male would presently return alone, and as the precautions now being taken by the people on the left bank were making it difficult for him to procure a human kill, he would probably try to cross over to the right bank of the Alaknanda, so for the next few nights I mounted guard on the Rudraprayag bridge.

Of the approaches to the bridge on the left bank, the one from the south passed close to the bridge *chowkidar's* house, and on the fourth night I heard the leopard killing the *chowkidar's* dog; a friendly nondescript little beast that used to run out and greet me every time I passed that way. The dog seldom barked, but that night it had been barking for five minutes when suddenly the bark ended in a yelp, followed by the shouting of the *chowkidar* from inside his house, after which there was silence. The thornbushes had been removed from the archway and the bridge was open, yet though I lay with finger on trigger for the rest of the night the leopard did not try to cross.

After killing the dog and leaving it lying on the road, the leopard, as I found from his tracks next morning, came to the tower. Five more steps in the direction in which he was going would have brought him out on the bridge, but those five steps he did not take. Instead he turned to the right, and after going a short distance up the footpath towards the bazaar, he returned and went up the pilgrim road to the north. A mile up the road I lost his tracks.

Two days later I received a report that a cow had been killed the previous evening, seven miles up the pilgrim road. It was suspected that the cow had been killed by the man-eater, for the previous night-—the night the dog had been killed—the leopard had tried to break open the door of a house close to where, the next evening, the cow had been killed.

On the road I found a number of men waiting for me who, knowing that the walk up from Rudraprayag would be a hot one, had very thoughtfully provided a dish of tea. While we sat in the shade of a mango- tree and smoked, and I drank the dish of tea, they told me that the cow had not returned with the herd the previous evening, and that it had been found between the road and the river when a search had been made for it that morning. They also told me of the many hairbreadth escapes each of them had had from the man-eater during the past eight years. I was very interested to learn from them that the leopard had only adopted his present habit of trying—and in many cases succeeding—to break open the doors of houses three years previously, and that before he had been content to take people who were outside their houses, or from houses the doors of which had been left open. 'Now,' they said, 'the shaitan has become so bold that sometimes when he has not been able to break down the door of a house, he has dug a hole through the mud wall, and got at his victims in the way.'

To those who do not know our hill-people, or understand their fear of the supernatural, it will seem incredible that a people renowned for their courage, and who have won the highest awards on the field of battle, should permit a leopard to break open a door, or to dig a hole in a wall of a house, in which in many cases there must have been men with axes, *kukris*, or, even in some cases, firearms at hand. I know of only one case in all those eight long years in which resistance was offered to the man- eater, and in that case the resister was a woman. She was sleeping alone in a house, the door of which she had left unfastened; this door, as in the case of the door of the house occupied by the woman who escaped with a lacerated arm, opened inwards. On entering the room the leopard seized the woman's left leg, and as it dragged her across the room, the woman's hand came in contact with a *gandesa*—a tool used for chopping chaff for cattle—and with this the woman dealt the leopard a blow. The leopard did not release his hold, but backed out of the room, and as it did so either the woman pushed the door, or else this happened accidentally. Whichever it may have been, with the woman on one side of the door and the leopard on the other, the leopard exerted its great strength and tore the limb from the woman's body. Mukandi Lai, at that time Member for Garhwal in the United Provinces Legislative Council, who was on an electioneering tour, arrived in the village the following day and spent a night in the room, but the leopard did not return. In a report to the Council, Mukandi Lai stated that seventy-five human beings had been killed by the leopard in the course of that one year, and he asked the Government to launch a vigorous campaign against the man-eater.

Accompanied by one of the villagers to show me the way, and by Madho Singh, I went down to the kill. 'Ihe cow had been killed in a deep ravine a quarter of a mile from the road and a hundred yards from the river. On one side of the ravine there were big rocks with dense brushwood between, and on the other side of the ravine there were a few small trees, none of which was big enough to sit in. Under the trees, and about thirty yards from the kill, there was a rock with a little hollow at the base of it, so in the hollow I decided to sit.

Both Madho Singh and the villager objected very strongly to my sitting on the ground, but as this was the first animal kill I had got since my arrival at Rudraprayag in a place where it was reasonable to expect the leopard to come at an early hour—about sundown—I overruled their objections, and sent them back to the village.

My seat was dry and comfortable, and with my back to the rock and a small bush to conceal my legs I was confident the leopard would not see me, and that I should be able to kill it before it was aware of my presence. I had provided myself with a torch and a knife, and with my good rifle across my knees I felt that in this secluded spot my chances of killing the leopard were better than any I had yet had.

Without movement and with my eyes on the rocks in front of me I sat through the evening, each second bringing the time nearer when the undisturbed and unsuspecting leopard would for a certainty return to his kill. The time I had been waiting for had come, and was passing. Objects near at hand were beginning to get blurred and indistinct. The leopard was a little later in coming than I had expected him to be, but that was not worrying me, for I had a torch, and the kill was only thirty yards from me, and I would be careful over my shot and make quite sure that I did not have a wounded animal to deal with.

In the deep ravine there was absolute silence. The hot sun of the past few days had made the dead leaves on the bank on which I was sitting as dry as tinder. This was very reassuring, for it was now dark and whereas previously I had depended on my eyes for protection I now had to depend on my ears, and with thumb on the button of the torch and finger on trigger I was prepared to shoot in any direction in which I heard the slightest sound.

The non-appearance of the leopard was beginning to cause me uneasiness. Was it possible that from some concealed place among the rocks he had been watching me all these hours, and was he now licking his lips in anticipation of burying his teeth in my throat?—for he had long been deprived of human flesh. In no other way could I account for his not having come, and if I were to have the good fortune to leave the ravine on my feet, my ears would have to serve me now as they had never served me before.

For what seemed like hours I strained my ears and then, noticing it was getting darker than it should have been, I turned my eyes up to the sky and saw that a heavy bank of clouds was drifting across the sky, obscuring the stars one by one. Shortly thereafter big drops of rain started to fall, and where there had been absolute and complete silence there was now sound and movement all round—the opportunity the leopard had been waiting for had come. Hastily taking off my coat I wound it round my neck, fastening it securely in place with the sleeves. The rifle was now useless but might help to cause a diversion, so transferring it to my left hand I unsheathed my knife and got a good grip of it with my right hand. The knife was what is called an Afridi stabbing knife, and I devoutly hoped it would serve me as well as it had served its late owner, for when buying it from the Government store at Hangu on the North-west Frontier, the Deputy Commissioner had drawn my attention to a label attached to it and to three notches on the handle, and said it had figured in three murders. Admittedly a gruesome relic, but I was glad to have it in my hand, and I clutched it tight while the rain lashed down.

Leopards, that is ordinary forest leopards, do not like rain and invariably seek shelter, but the man-eater was not an ordinary leopard, and there was no knowing what his likes or dislikes were, or what he might or might not do.

When Madho Singh was leaving he asked how long I intended sitting up, and I had answered, 'Until I have shot the leopard', so I could expect no help from him, and of help I was at that time in urgent need. Should I go or should I remain were the questions that were troubling me, and one option was as unattractive as the other. If the leopard up to then had not seen me it would be foolish to give my position away, and possibly fall across him on the difficult ground I should have to negotiate on my way up to the pilgrim road. On the other hand to remain where I was for another six hours—momentarily expecting to have to fight for my life with an unfamiliar weapon—would put a strain on my nerves which they .were not capable of standing; so getting to my feet and shouldering the rifle, I set off.

I had not far to go, only about five hundred yards, half of which was over wet clay and the other half over rocks worn smooth by bare feet and the hooves of cattle. Afraid to use the torch for fear of attracting the man- eater, and with one hand occupied with the rifle and the other with the knife, my body made as many contacts with the ground as my rubber- shod feet. When I eventually reached the road I sent a full-throated cooee into the night, and a moment later I saw a door in the village far up the hillside open and Madho Singh and his companion emerge, carrying a lantern.

When the two men joined me Madho Singh said he had had no uneasiness about me until the rain started, and that he had then lit the lantern, and sat with his ear against the door listening. Both men were willing to accompany me back to Rudraprayag, so we set out on our seven-mile walk, Bachi Singh leading, Madho Singh carrying the lantern following, and I bringing up the rear. When I returned next day I found the kill had not been touched, and on the road I found the tracks of the man-eater. What time had elapsed between our going down the road and the man-eater following us, it was not possible to say.

When I look back on that night, I look back on it as my night of terror. I have been frightened times without number, but never have I been frightened as I was that night when the unexpected rain came down and robbed me of all my defences, and left me for protection a murderer's knife.

LEOPARD FIGHTS LEOPARD

After following us to Rudraprayag the leopard went down the pilgrim road through Golabrai, past the ravine up which he had gone a few days previously, and then up a rough track which the people living on the hills to the east of Rudraprayag use as a short cut on their way to and from Hardwar.

The pilgrimage to Kedarnath and Badrinath is seasonal, and the commencement of the pilgrimage and its duration depend in the one case on the melting and in the other on the falling of snow in the upper reaches of the high mountains in which these two shrines are situated. The High Priest of Badrinath temple had a few days previously sent the telegram that is eagerly awaited by good Hindus throughout the length and breadth of India, announcing that the road was open, and for the past few days pilgrims in small numbers had been passing through Rudraprayag.

During the past few years the man-eater had killed several pilgrims on the road, and it appeared to be his more or less regular habit while the pilgrim season lasted to go down the road to the extent of his beat, and then circle round through the villages on the hills to the east of Rudraprayag, and rejoin the road anything up to fifteen miles above Rudraprayag. The time taken for this round trip varied, but on an average I had seen the leopard's tracks on the stretch of road between Rudraprayag and Golabrai once in every five days, so on my way back to the Inspection Bungalow I selected a place from where I could overlook the road, and for the next two nights sat in great comfort on a hayrick, without however seeing anything of the leopard.

I received no news of the man-eater from outlying villages for two days, and on the third morning I went down the pilgrim road for six miles to try to find out if he had recently visited any of the villages in the direction. From this twelve-mile walk I returned at midday, and while I was having a late breakfast two men arrived and reported that a boy had been killed the previous evening at Bhainswara, a village eighteen miles south-east of Rudraprayag.

The intelligence system introduced by Ibbotson was working splendidly. Under this system cash rewards, on a graduated scale, were paid for information about all kills in the area in which the man-eater was " operating. These rewards, starting with two rupees for a goat and working up to twenty rupees for a human being, were keenly contested for, and so ensured our receiving information about all kills in the shortest time possible.

When I put ten rupees into the hands of each of the men who had brought me news about the boy, one of them offered to accompany me back to Bhainswara to show me the way, while the other said he would stay the night at Rudraprayag as he had recently had fever and could not do another eighteen miles that day. I finished breakfast while the men were telling me their tale, and a little before 1 p.m. I set off, taking only my rifle, a few cartridges, and a torch with me. As we crossed the road near the Inspection Bungalow and started up the steep hill on the far side of it, my companion informed me we had a very long way to go, adding that it would not be safe for us to be out after dark, so I told him to walk ahead and set the pace. I never—if I can help it—walk uphill immediately after a meal, but here I had no option, and for the first three miles, in which we climbed four thousand feet, I had great difficulty in keeping up with my guide. A short stretch of comparatively flat ground at the end of the three miles gave me back my wind, and after that I walked ahead and set the pace.

On their way to Rudraprayag the two men had told the people in the villages they had passed through about the kill, and of their intention to try and persuade me to accompany them back to Bhainswara. I do not think that anyone doubted that I would answer to the call, for at every village the entire population were waiting for me, and while some gave me their blessings, others begged me not to leave the district until I had killed their enemy.

My companion had assured me that we had eighteen miles to go, and as we crested hill after hill with deep valleys between I realized I had undertaken to walk against time eighteen of the longest and hardest miles I had ever walked. The sun was near setting when, from the crest of one of these unending hills, I saw a number of men standing on a ridge a few hundred yards ahead of us. On catching sight of us some of the men disappeared over the ridge, while others came forward to meet us. The Headman of Bhainswara was among the latter, and after he had greeted me, he cheered me by telling me that his village was just over the crest of the hill, and that he had sent his son back to get tea ready.

The 14th of April 1926 is a date that will long be remembered in Garhwal, for it was on that day that the man-eating leopard of Rudraprayag killed'his last human victim. On the evening of that day a widow and her two children, a girl aged nine and a boy aged twelve, accompanied by a neighbour's son aged eight, went to a spring a few yards from Bhainswara village to draw water for the preparation of their evening meal.

The widow and her children occupied a house in the middle of a long row of homesteads. These homesteads were double-storied, the low- ceilinged ground floor being used for the storage of grain and fuel, and the first floor for residences. A verandah four feet wide ran the entire length of the building, and short flights of stone steps flanked by walls gave access to the verandah, each flight of steps being used by two families. A flagged courtyard, sixty feet wide and three hundred feet long, bordered by a low wall, extended along the whole length of the building.

The neighbour's son was leading as the party of four approached the steps used by the widow and her children, and as the boy started to mount the steps he saw an animal, which he mistook for a dog, lying in an open room on the ground floor adjoining the steps; he said nothing about the animal at the time, and the others apparently did not see it. The boy was followed by the girl, the widow came next, and her son brought up the rear. When she was halfway up the short flight of stone steps, the mother heard the heavy brass vessel her son was carrying crash on the steps and go rolling down them; reprimanding him for his carelessness, she set her own vessel down on the verandah and turned to see what damage her son had done. At the bottom of the steps she saw the overturned vessel. She went down and picked it up, and then looked round for her son. As he was nowhere in sight she assumed he had got frightened and had run away, so she started calling to him.

Neighbours in adjoining houses had heard the noise made by the falling vessel and now, hearing the mother calling to her son, they came to their doors and asked what all the trouble was about. It was suggested that the boy might be hiding in one of the ground-floor rooms, so as it was now getting dark in these rooms, a man lit a lantern and came down the steps towards the woman, and as he did so he saw drops of blood on the flagstones where the woman was standing. At the sound of the man's horrified ejaculation other people descended into the courtyard, among whom was an old man who had accompanied his master on many shooting expeditions. Taking the lantern from the owner's hand, this old man followed the blood trail across the courtyard and over the low wall. Beyond the wall was a drop of eight feet into a yam field; here in the soft earth were the splayed-out pugmarks of a leopard. Up to that moment no •one suspected that the boy had been carried off by a man-eater, for though everyone had heard about the leopard it had never previously been within ten miles of their village. As soon as they realized what had happened the women began screaming and while some men ran to their houses for drums, others ran for guns—of which there were three in the village—and in a few minutes pandemonium broke out. Throughout the night drums were beaten and guns were fired. At daylight the boy's body was recovered, and two men were dispatched to Rudraprayag to inform me.

As I approached the village in company with the Headman, I heard the wailing of a woman mourning her dead. It was the mother of the victim, and she was the first to greet me. Even to my unpractised eye it was apparent that the bereaved mother had just weathered one hysterical storm and was heading for another, and as

I lack the art of dealing with people in this condition I was anxious to spare the woman a recital of the events of the previous evening; but she appeared to be eager to give me her version of the story, so I let her have her way. As the story unfolded itself it was apparent that her object in telling it was to ventilate her grievance against the men of the village for not having run after the leopard and rescued her son 'as his father would have done had he been alive'. In her accusation against the men I told her she was unjust, and in her belief that her son could have been rescued alive, I told her she was wrong. For when the leopard clamped his teeth round the boy's throat, the canine teeth dislocated the head from the neck and the boy was already dead before the leopard carried him across the courtyard, and nothing the assembled men—or anyone else—could have done would have been of any use.

Standing in the courtyard drinking the tea that had thoughtfully been provided for me, and noting the hundred or more people who were gathered round, it was difficult to conceive how an animal the size of a leopard had crossed the courtyard in daylight without being seen by any of the people who must have been moving about at that time, or how its presence had gone undetected by the dogs in the village.

I climbed down the eight-foot wall that the leopard carrying the boy had jumped down, and followed the drag across the yam field, down another wall twelve feet high, and across another field. At the edge of this second field there was a thick hedge of rambler roses, four feet high. Here the leopard had released his hold on the boy's throat, and after searching for an opening in the hedge and not finding one, he had picked the boy up by the small of the back and, leaping the hedge, gone down a wall ten feet high on the far side. There was a cattle track at the foot of this third • wall and the leopard had only gone a short distance along it when the alarm was raised in the village. The leopard had then dropped the boy on the cattle track and gone down the hill. He was prevented from returning to his kill by the beating of drums and the firing of guns which had gone on all night in the village.

The obvious thing for me to have done would have been to carry the body of the boy back to where the leopard had left it, and to have sat over it there. But here I was faced with two difficulties—the absence of a suitable place in which to sit, and my aversion to sitting in an unsuitable place.

The nearest tree, a leafless walnut, was three hundred yards away, and was therefore out of the question, and quite frankly I lacked the courage to sit on the ground. I had arrived at the village at sundown; it had taken a little time to drink the tea, hear the mothers story, and trail the leopard, and there was not sufficient daylight left for me to construct a shelter that would have given me even the semblance of protection; therefore if I sat on the ground I should have to sit just anywhere, not knowing from which direction the leopard would come, and knowing full well that if the leopard attacked me 1 should get no opportunity of using the one weapon with which I was familiar, my rifle, for when in actual contact with an unwounded leopard or tiger it is not possible to use firearms.

When after my tour of inspection I returned to the courtyard, I asked the Headman for a crowbar, a stout wooden peg, a hammer, and a dog chain. With the crowbar I prised up one of the flagstones in the middle of the courtyard, drove the peg firmly into the ground, and fastened one end of the chain to it. Then with the help of the Headman I carried the body of the boy to the peg and chained it there.

The working of the intangible force which sets a period to life, which one man calls Fate and another calls kismet, is incomprehensible. During the past few days this force had set a period to the life of a breadwinner, leaving his family destitute; had ended in a very painful way the days of an old lady who after a lifetime of toil was looking forward to a few short years of comparative comfort; and now, had cut short the life of this boy who, by the look of him, had been nurtured with care by his widowed mother. Small wonder then that the bereaved mother should, in between her hysterical crying, be repeating over and over and over again, 'What crime, *Parmeshwar*, has my son, who was loved by all, committed that on the threshold of life he has deserved death in this terrible way?'

Before prising up the flagstone, I had asked for the mother and her daughter to be taken to a room at the very end of the row of buildings. My preparations completed, I washed at the spring and asked for a bundle of straw, which I laid on the verandah in front of the door of the house vacated by the mother.

Darkness had now fallen. Having asked the assembled people to be as silent during the night as it was possible for them to be and sent them to their respective homes, I took up my position on the verandah, where by lying prone on my side and heaping a little straw in front, I could get a clear view of the kill without much chance of being seen myself.

In spite of all the noise that had been made the previous night, I had a feeling that the leopard would return, and that when he failed to find his kill where he had left it, he would come to the village to try to secure another victim. The ease with which he had got his first victim at Bhainswara would encourage him to try again, and I started my vigil with high hopes.

Heavy clouds had been gathering all the evening, and at 8 p.m., when all the village sound—except the wailing of the woman—were hushed, a flash of lightning followed by a distant roll of thunder heralded an approaching storm. For an hour the storm raged, the lightning being so continuous and brilliant that had a rat ventured into the courtyard I should have seen and probably been able to shoot it. The rain eventually stopped but, the sky remaining overcast, visibility was reduced to a few inches. The time had now come for the leopard to start from wherever he had been sheltering from the storm, and the time of his arrival would depend on the distance of that place from the village.

The woman had now stopped wailing, and in all the world there appeared to be no sound. This was as I had hoped, for all I had to warn me that the leopard had come were my ears, and to help them I had used the dog chain instead of a rope.

The straw that had been provided for me was as dry as tinder and my ears, straining into the black darkness, first heard the sound when it was level with my feet—something was creeping, very stealthily creeping, over the straw on which I was lying. I was wearing an article of clothing called shorts, which left my legs bare in the region of my knees. Presently, against this bare skin, I felt the hairy coat of an animal brushing. It could only be the man-eater, creeping up until he could lean over and get a grip of my throat. A little pressure now on my left shoulder—to get a foothold— and then, just as I was about to press the trigger of the rifle to cause a diversion, a small animal jumped down between my arms and my chest. It was a little kitten, soaking wet, that had been caught out in the storm and, finding every door shut, had come to me for warmth and protection.

The kitten had hardly made itself comfortable inside my coat, and I was just beginning to recover from the fright it had given me, when from beyond the terraced fields there was some low growling which gradually grew louder, and then merged into the most savage fight I have ever heard. Quite evidently the man-eater had returned to the spot where the previous night he had left his kill, and while he was searching for it, in not too good a temper, another male leopard who looked upon this particular area as his hunting-ground, had accidentally come across him and set on him. Fights of the nature of the one that was taking place in my hearing are very unusual, for carnivores invariably keep to their own areas, and if by chance two of a sex happen to meet, they size up each other's capabilities at a glance, and the weaker gives way to the stronger.

The man-eater, though old, was a big and a very powerful male, and in the five hundred square miles he ranged over there was possibly no other male capable of disputing his rule, but here at Bhainswara he was a stranger and a trespasser, and to get out of the trouble he had brought on himself he would have to fight for his life. And this he was undoubtedly doing.

My chance of getting a shot had now gone, for even if the man-eater succeeded in defeating his attacker, his injuries would probably prevent him from taking any interest in kills for some time to come. There was even a possibility of the fight ending fatally for him, and here would indeed be an unexpected end to his career: killed in an accidental encounter by one of his own kind, when the combined efforts of the Government and the public had failed, over a period of eight years, to accomplish this end.

The first round, lasting about five minutes, was fought with unabating savagery, and was inconclusive, for at the end of it I could still hear both animals. After an interval of ten or fifteen minutes the fight was resumed, but at a distance of two to three hundred yards from where it had originally started; quite evidently the local champion was getting the better of the fight and was gradually driving the intruder out of the ring. The third round was shorter than the two that had preceded it, but was no less savage, and when after another long period of silence the fight was again resumed, the scene had receded to the shoulder of the hill, where after a few minutes it died out of hearing.

There were still six hours of darkness left; even so I knew my mission to Bhainswara had failed, and that my hope that the fight would be fought to a .finish and would end in the death of the man-eater had been short¬lived. In the running fight into which the contest had now degenerated the man-eater would sustain injuries, but they were not likely to reduce his craving for human flesh or impair his ability to secure it.

The kitten slept peacefully throughout the night, and as the first streak of dawn showed in the east I descended into the courtyard and carried the boy to the shed from where we had removed him, and covered him with the blanket which previously had been used for the purpose. The Headman was still asleep when I knocked on his door. I declined the tea, which I knew would take some time to make, and assured him that the man-eater would never again visit his village; and when he had promised to make immediate arrangements to have the boy carried to the burning- ghat, I set off on my long walk back to Rudraprayag.

No matter how often we fail in any endeavour, we never get used to the feeling of depression that assails us after each successive failure. Day after day over a period of months I had left the Inspection Bungalow full of hope that on this particular occasion I would meet with success, and day after day I had returned disappointed and depressed. Had my failures only concerned myself they would not have mattered, but in the task I had undertaken those failures concerned others more than they concerned me. Bad luck—for to nothing else could I attribute my failures—was being meted out to me in ever-increasing measure, and the accumulated effect was beginning to depress me and give me the feeling that I was not destined to do what I had set out to do. What but bad luck had made the man-eater drop his kill where there were no trees? And what but bad luck had made a leopard who possibly had thirty square miles in which to wander, arrive at a particular spot in those thirty miles just as the man- eater, not finding his kill where he had left it, was quite conceivably on his way to the village where I was waiting for him?

The eighteen miles had been long yesterday but they were longer today, and the hills were steeper. In the villages I passed through the people were eagerly awaiting me, and though I only had bad news they did not show their disappointment. Their boundless faith in their philosophy, a faith strong enough to move mountains and very soothing to depressed feelings, that no human beings and no animals can die before their appointed time, and that the man-eater's time had not yet come, called for no explanation, and admitted of no argument.

Ashamed of the depression and feeling of frustration that I had permitted to accompany me throughout the morning, I left the last f village—where I had been made to halt and drink a cup of tea—greatly cheered, and as I swung down the last four miles to Rudraprayag I became aware that I was treading on the pugmarks of the man-eater. Strange how one's mental condition can dull, or sharpen, one's powers of observation. The man-eater had quite possibly joined the track many miles farther back, and now, after my conversation with the simple village-folk—and a drink of tea—I was seeing his pugmarks for the first time that morning. The track here ran over red clay which the rain had softened, and the pug marks of the man-eater showed that he was walking at his accustomed pace. Half a mile farther on he started to quicken his pace, and this pace he continued to maintain until he reached the head of the ravine above Golabrai; down this ravine the leopard had gone.

When a leopard or tiger is walking at its normal pace only the imprints of the hind feet are seen, but when the normal pace is for any reason exceeded, the hind feet are placed on the ground in advance of the forefeet, and thus the imprints of all four feet are seen. From the distance between the imprints of the fore and the hind feet it is possible to determine the speed at which an animal of the cat tribe was travelling. The coming of daylight would in this instance have been sufficient reason for the man- eater to have quickened his pace.

I had previously had experience of the man-eater's walking capabilities, but only when ranging his beat in search of food. Here he had a better reason for the long walk he had undertaken, for he was anxious to put as great a distance as possible between himself and the leopard who had given him a lesson in the law of trespass; how severe that lesson had been will be apparent from a description given later.

A SHOT IN THE DARK

Mealtimes in India vary according to the season of the year and individual tastes. In most establishments the recognized times for the three principal meals are: breakfast, 8 to 9; lunch, 1 to 2; and dinner, 8 to 9. During all the months I was at Rudraprayag my mealtimes were very erratic, and contrary to the accepted belief that health depends on the composition and regularity of meals, my unorthodox and irregular meals kept me fighting fit. Porridge supped at 8 p.m., soup taken at 8 a.m., one combined meal in the day or no meal at all, appeared to have no injurious effect beyond taking a little flesh off my bones.

I had eaten nothing since my breakfast the previous day, so as I intended spending the night out I had a nondescript meal on my return from Bhainswara, and after an hour's sleep and a bath set off for Golabrai to warn the *pundit* who owned the pilgrim shelter of the presence in his vicinity of the man-eater.

I had made friends with the *pundit* on my first arrival at Rudraprayag and I never passed his house without having a few words with him, for in addition to the many interesting tales he had to tell about the man-eater and the pilgrims who passed through Golabrai, he was one of the only two people—the woman who escaped with the lacerated arm being the other—whom I met during my stay in Garhwal who had survived an encounter with the man-eater.

One of his tales concerned a woman who had lived in a village further down the road, and with whom he had been acquainted. After a visit to the Rudraprayag bazaar one day this woman arrived at Golabrai late in the evening, and fearing she would not be able to reach her home before dark she asked the *pundit* to let her spend the night in his shelter. This he permitted her to do advising her to sleep in front of the door of the storeroom in which he kept the articles of food purchased by the pilgrims, for, he said, she would then be protected by the room on the one side, and by the fifty or more pilgrims who were spending the night in the shelter on the other.

The shelter was a grass shed open on the side nearest the road, and boarded up on the side nearest the hill; the store-room was midway along the shed, but was recessed into the hill and did not obstruct the floor of the shed, so when the woman lay down at the door of the store-room there were rows of pilgrims between her and the road. Some time during the night one of the women pilgrims screamed out and said she had been stung by a scorpion. No lights were available, but with the help of matches the woman's foot was examined and a small scratch from which a little blood was flowing was found on her foot. Grumbling that the woman had made a lot of fuss about nothing, and that in any case blood did not flow from a scorpion sting, the pilgrims soon composed themselves and resumed their sleep.

In the morning, when the *pundit* arrived from his house on the hill above the mango tree, he saw a sari worn by hill-women lying on the road in front of the shelter, and on the sari there was blood. The *pundit* had given his friend what he considered to be the safest place in the shelter, and with fifty or more pilgrims lying all round her the leopard had walked over the sleeping people, killed the woman, and accidentally scratched the sleeping pilgrim's foot when returning to the road. The explanation given by the *pundit* as to why the leopard had rejected the pilgrims and carried off the hill-woman was that she was the only person in the shelter that night who was wearing a coloured garment. This explanation is not convincing, and but for the fact that leopards do not hunt by scent, my own explanation would have been that of all the people in the shelter the hill-woman was the only one who had a familiar smell. Was it just bad luck, or fate, or being the only one of all the sleepers who realized the danger of sleeping in an open shed? Had the victim's fear in some inexplicable way conveyed itself to the man-eater, and attracted him to her?

It was not long after this occurrence that the *pundit* had his own encounter with the man-eater. The exact date—which could if desired be ascertained from the hospital records at Rudraprayag—is immaterial, and for the purpose of my story it will be sufficient to say that it took place during the hottest part of the summer of 1921, that is four years before I met the *pundit*. Late one evening of that summer ten pilgrims from Madras arrived weary and footsore at Golabrai, and expressed their intention of spending the night in the pilgrim shelter. Fearing that if any more people were killed at Golabrai his shelter would get a bad reputation, the *pundit* tried to persuade them to continue on for another two miles to Rudraprayag, where they would be ensured of safe accommodation.

Finding that nothing he could say had any effect on the tired pilgrims, he finally consented to give them accommodation in his house, which was fifty yards above the mango-tree to which I have already drawn attention. • The *pundit*'s house was built on the same plan as the homesteads at Bhainswara; a low ground-floor room used for storage of fuel, and a first- floor room used as a residence. A short flight of stone steps gave access to a narrow verandah, the door of the residential room being opposite to the landing at the top of the steps.

After the *pundit* and the ten guests that had been forced on him had eaten their evening meal, they locked themselves into the room, which was not provided with any means of ventilation. The heat in the room was stifling, and fearing that he would be suffocated the *pundit* some time during the night opened the door, stepped outside, and stretched his hands to the pillars on either side of the steps supporting the roof of the verandah. As he did so and filled his lungs with the night air, his throat was gripped as in a vice. Retaining his hold on the pillars, he got the soles of his feet against the body of his assailant and with a desperate kick tore the leopard's teeth from his throat, and hurled it down the steps. Then, fearing that he was going to faint, he took a step sideways and supported himself by putting both hands on the railing of the verandah, and the moment he did so the leopard sprang up from below and buried its claws in his left forearm. The downward pull was counteracted by the railing on which the *pundit* had the palm of his hand, and the weight of the leopard caused its sharp claws to rip through the flesh of his arm until they tore free at his wrist. Before the leopard was able to spring a second time, the pilgrims, hearing the terrifying sounds the *pundit* was making in his attempts to breathe through the gap torn in his throat, dragged him into the room and bolted the door. For the rest of that long hot night the *pundit* lay gasping for breath and bleeding profusely, while the leopard growled and clawed at the frail door, and the pilgrims screamed with terror.

At daylight the pilgrims carried the *pundit*, now mercifully unconscious, to a Kalakamli hospital at Rudraprayag, where for three months he was fed through a silver tube inserted in his throat. After an absence of over six months he returned to his home in Golabrai, broken in health and with his hair turned grey. Photographs were taken five years later, and scarcely show the leopard's teeth-marks on the left side of the *pundit*'s face and in his throat, and its claw-marks on his left arm, though they were still clearly visible.

In his conversations with me the *pundit* always referred to the man- eater as an evil spirit, and after the first day, when he had asked me what proof I could give him in face of his own experience that evil spirits could not assume material form, I also, to humour him, referred to the man- eater as 'the evil spirit'.

On arrival at Golabrai that evening I told the *pundit* of my fruitless visit to Bhainswara, and warned him to take extra precautions for his safety and for the safety of any pilgrims who might be staying in his shelter; for the evil spirit, after its long excursion into the hills, had now returned to the vicinity.

That night, and for the following three nights, I sat on the haystack, keeping a watch on the road; and on the fourth day Ibbotson returned from Pauri.

Ibbotson always infused new life into me, for his creed, like that of the locals, was that no one was to blame if the man-eater had not died yesterday, for surely it would die today or maybe tomorrow. I had a lot to tell him, for though I had corresponded with him regularly—extracts from my letters being embodied in his reports to the Government, and by them made available to the press—I had not been able to give him all the details which he was now eager to hear. On his part Ibbotson also had a lot to tell me; this concerned the clamour being made in the press for the destruction of the man-eater, and the suggestion that sportsmen from all parts of India be encouraged to go to Garhwal to assist in killing the leopard. This press campaign had resulted in Ibbotson receiving only one inquiry, and only one suggestion. The inquiry was from a sportsman who said that, if arrangements for his travel, accommodation, food, and so on, were made to his satisfaction, he would consider whether it was worth his while to come to Golabrai; and the suggestion was from a sportsman in whose opinion the speediest and easiest way of killing the leopard was to paint a goat over with arsenic, sew up its mouth to prevent it licking itself, and then tie it up in a place where the leopard would find and eat it, and so poison itself.

We talked long that day, reviewing my many failures in minutest detail, and by lunch-time, when I had told Ibbotson of the leopard's habit of going down the road between Rudraprayag and Golabrai on an average once in every five days, I convinced him that the only hope I now had of shooting the leopard was by sitting over the road for ten nights, for, as I pointed out to him, the leopard would be almost certain to use the road at least once during the period. Ibbotson consented to my plan very reluctantly, for I had already sat up many nights and he was afraid that another ten on end would be too much for me. However, I carried my point, and then told Ibbotson that if I did not succeed in killing the leopard within the stipulated time, I would return to Naini Tal and leave the field free for any new-comers who might consider it worth their while to take my place.

That evening Ibbotson accompanied me to Golabrai and helped me to put up a *machan* in the mango tree a hundred yards from the pilgrim shelter and fifty yards below the *pundit*'s house. Immediately below the tree, and in the middle of the road, we drove a stout wooden peg, and to this peg we tethered a goat with a small bell round its neck. The moon was nearly at its full; even so, the high hill to the east of Golabrai only admitted of the moon lighting up the deep Ganges valley for a few hours, and if the leopard came while it was dark the goat would warn me of his approach.

When all our preparations had been made Ibbotson returned to the bungalow, promising to send two of my men for me early next morning. While I sat on a rock near the foot of the tree and smoked and waited for night to close in, the *pundit* came and sat down beside me; he was a bhakti and did not smoke. Earlier in the evening he had seen us building the *machan*, and he now tried to dissuade me from sitting all night in the tree when I could sleep comfortably in bed. Nevertheless, I assured him I would sit all that night in the tree, and for nine nights thereafter, for if I was not able to kill the evil spirit I could at least guard his house and the pilgrim shelter from attack by all enemies. Once during the night a *kakar* barked on the hill above me, but thereafter the night was silent. At sunrise next morning two of my men arrived, and I set off for the Inspection Bungalow, examining the road as I went for pugmarks, and leaving the men to follow with my rug and rifle.

During the following nine days my programme did not vary. Leaving the bungalow accompanied by two men in the early evening, I took up my position in the *machan* and sent the men away in time for them to get back to the bungalow before dusk. The men had strict orders not to leave the bungalow before it was fully light, and they arrived each morning as the sun was rising on the hills on the far side of the river and accompanied me back to the bungalow.

During all those ten nights the barking of the *kakar* on the first night was all that I heard. That the man-eater was still in the vicinity we had ample proof, for twice within those ten nights it had broken into houses and carried off, on the first occasion, a goat and, on the second occasion, a sheep. I found both kills with some difficulty for they had been carried a long distance, but neither had been of any use to me as they had been eati^n out. Once also during those ten nights the leopard had broken down the door of a house which, fortunately for the inmates, had two rooms, the door of the inner room being sufficiently strong to withstand the leopard's onslaught.

On return to the bungalow after my tenth night in the mango tree, Ibbotson and I discussed our future plans. No further communications had been received from the sportsman, no one else had expressed a desire to accept the Government's invitation, and no one had responded to the appeals made by the press. Neither Ibbotson nor I could afford to spend more time at Rudraprayag; Ibbotson because he had been away from his headquarters for ten days and it was necessary for him to return to Pauri to attend to urgent work; and I because I had work to do in Africa and had delayed my departure for three months and could not delay it any longer. Both of us were reluctant to leave Garhwal to the tender mercies of the man-eater and yet, situated as we were, it was hard to decide what to do. One solution was for Ibbotson to apply for leave, and for me to cancel my passage to Africa and cut my losses. We finally agreed to leave the decision over for that night, and to decide on our line of action next morning. Having come to this decision I told Ibbotson I would spend my last night in Garhwal in the mango tree.

Ibbotson accompanied me on that eleventh, and last, evening, and as we approached Golabrai we saw a number of men standing on the side of the road, looking down into a field a little beyond the mango-tree; the men had not seen us and before we got up to them they turned and moved off towards the pilgrim shelter. One of them however looked back, and seeing me beckoning retraced his steps. In answer to our questions he said he and his companions had for an hour been watching a great fight between two big snakes down in the field. No crops appeared to have been grown there for a year or more, and the snakes had last been seen near the big rock in the middle of the field. There were smears of blood on this rock, and the man said they had been made by the snakes, which had bitten each other and were bleeding in several places. Having broken a stick from a nearby bush, I jumped down into the field to see if there were any holes near the rock, and as I did so I caught sight of the snakes in a bush just below the road. Ibbotson had in the meantime armed himself with a stout stick, and as one of the snakes tried to climb up on to the road he killed it. The other one disappeared into a hole in the bank from where we were unable to dislodge it. The snake Ibbotson had killed was about seven feet long and of a uniform light straw colour, and on its neck it had several bites. It was not a rat snake, and as it had very pronounced poison fangs we concluded it was some variety of hoodless cobra. Cold-blooded creatures are not immune to snake poison, for I have seen a frog bitten by a cobra die in a few minutes, but I do not know if snakes of the same variety can poison each other, and the one that escaped into the hole may have died in a few minutes or it may have lived to die of old age.

After Ibbotson left, the *pundit* passed under my tree on his way to the pilgrim shelter, carrying a pail of milk. He informed me that a hundred and fifty pilgrims, who had arrived during the day, were determined to spend the night in his shelter and that he was powerless to do anything about it. It was then too late for me to take any action, so I told him to warn the pilgrims to keep close together and not on any account to move about after dark. When he hurried back to his house a few minutes later, he said he had warned the pilgrims accordingly.

In a field adjoining the road, and about a hundred yards from my tree, there was a thorn enclosure in which a packman—not my old friend— earlier in the evening had penned his flock of goats and sheep. With the packman were two dogs who had barked very fiercely at us as we came down the road, and at Ibbotson after he left me to go back to the bungalow.

The moon was a few days past the full, and the valley was in darkness when, a little after 9 p.m., I saw a man carrying a lantern leave the pilgrim shelter and cross the road. A minute or two later, he recrossed the road and on gaining the shelter extinguished the lantern and at the same moment the packman's dogs started barking furiously. The dogs were unmistakably barking at a leopard, which quite possibly had seen the man with the lantern and was now coming down the road on its way to the shelter.

At first the dogs barked in the direction of the road, but after a little while they turned and barked in my direction. The leopard had now quite evidently caught sight of the sleeping goat and lain down out of sight of the dogs—which had stopped barking—to consider his next move. I knew that the leopard had arrived, and I also knew that he was using my tree to stalk the goat, and the question that was tormenting me as the long minutes dragged by was whether he would skirt round the goat and kill one of the pilgrims, or whether he would kill the goat and give me a shot.

During all the nights I had sat in the tree I adopted a position that would enable me to discharge my rifle with the minimum of movement and in the minimum of time. The distance between the goat and my *machan* was about twenty feet, but the night was so dark under the dense ,' foliage of the tree that my straining eyes could not penetrate even this short distance, so I closed them and concentrated on my hearing.

My rifle, to which I had a small electric torch attached, was pointing in the direction of the goat, and I was just beginning to think that the leopard—assuming it was the man-eater—had reached the shelter and was selecting a human victim, when there was a rush from the foot of the tree, and the goat's bell tinkled sharply. Pressing the button of the torch I saw that the sights of the rifle were aligned on the shoulder of a leopard, and without having to move the rifle a fraction of an inch I pressed the trigger, and as I did so the torch went out.

Torches in those days were not in as general use as they are now, and mine was the first I had ever possessed. I had carried it for several months and never had occasion to use it, and I did not know the life of the battery, or that it was necessary to test it. When I pressed the button on this occasion the torch gave only one dim flash and then went out, and I was again in darkness without knowing what the result of my shot had been.

The echo of my shot was dying away in the valley when the *pundit* opened his door and called out to ask if I needed any help. I was at the time listening with all my ears for any sounds that might come from the leopard, so I did not answer him, and he hurriedly shut his door.

The leopard had been lying across the road with his head away from me when I fired, and I was vaguely aware of his having sprung over the goat and gone down the hillside, and just before the *pundit* had called I thought I heard what may have been a gurgling sound, but of this I could not be sure. The pilgrims had been aroused by my shot but, after murmuring for a few minutes, they resumed their sleep. The goat appeared to be unhurt, for from the sound of his bell I could tell that he was moving about and apparently eating the grass of which he was given a liberal supply each night.

I had fired my shot at 10 p.m. As the moon was not due to rise for several hours, and as there was nothing I could do in the meantime, I made myself comfortable, and listened and smoked.

Hours later the moon lit up the crest of the hills on the far side of the Ganges and slowly crept down into the valley, and a little later I saw it rise over the top of the hill behind me. As soon as it was overhead I climbed to the top of the tree, but found that the spreading branches impeded my view. Descending again to the *machan*, I climbed out on the branches spreading over the road, but from here also I found it was not possible to see down the hillside in the direction in which I thought the leopard had .'gone. It was then 3 a.m., and two hours later the moon began to pale. When nearby objects became visible in the light of the day that was being born in the east, I descended from the tree and was greeted by a friendly bleat from the goat.

Beyond the goat, and at the very edge of the road, there was a long low rock, and on this rock there was an inch-wide streak of blood; the leopard from which that blood had come could only have lived a minute or two, so dispensing with the precautions usually taken when following up the blood trail of carnivores, I scrambled down off the road and, taking up the trail on the far side of the rock, followed it for fifty yards, to where the leopard was lying dead. He had slid backwards into a hole in the ground, in which he was now lying crouched up, with his chin resting on the edge of the hole.

No marks by which I could identify the dead animal were visible, even so I never for one moment doubted that the leopard in the hole was the man-eater. But here was no fiend, who while watching me through the long night hours had rocked and rolled with silent fiendish laughter at my vain attempts to outwit him, and licked his lips in anticipation of the time when, finding me off my guard for one brief moment, he would get the opportunity he was waiting for of burying his teeth in my throat. Here was only an old leopard, who differed from others of his kind in that his muzzle was grey and his lips lacked whiskers; the best-hated and the most feared animal in all India, whose only crime—not against the laws of nature, but against the laws of man—was that he had shed human blood, with no object of terrorizing man, but only in order that he might live; and who now, with his chin resting on the rim of the hole and his eyes half-closed, was peacefully sleeping his long last sleep.

While I stood unloading my rifle, one bullet from which had more than cancelled my personal score against the sleeper, I heard a cough, and on looking up saw the *pundit* peering down at me from the edge of the road. I beckoned to him and he came gingerly down the hill. On catching sight of the leopard s head he stopped, and asked in a whisper whether it was dead, and what it was. When I told him it was dead, and that it was the evil spirit that had torn open his throat five years ago, and for fear of which he had hurriedly closed his door the previous night, he put his hands together and attempted to put his head on my feet. Next minute there was a call from the road above of, '*Sahib*, where are you?' It was one of my men calling in great agitation, and when I sent an answering call echoing over the Ganges, four heads appeared, and catching sight of ,us four men came helter-skelter down the hill, one of them swinging a lighted lantern which he had forgotten to extinguish.

The leopard had got stiff in the hole and was extracted with some little difficulty. While it was being tied to the stout bamboo pole the men had brought with them, they told me they had been unable to sleep that night and that as soon as Ibbotson's jemadar's watch showed them it was 4.30 a.m., they lit the lantern, and arming themselves with a pole and a length of rope had come to look for me, for they felt that I was in urgent need of them. Not finding me in the *machan* and seeing the goat unhurt, and the streak of blood on the rock, they concluded the man-eater had killed me, and not knowing what to do they had in desperation called to me.

Leaving the *pundit* to retrieve my rug from the *machan*, and give the pilgrims who were now crowding round his version of the night's happenings, the four men and I, with the goat trotting alongside, set off for the Inspection Bungalow. The goat, who had escaped with very little injury owing to my having fired the moment the leopard caught him, little knew that his night's adventure was to make him a hero for the rest of his life, and that he was to wear a fine brass collar and be a source of income to the man from whom I had purchased him, and to whom I gave him back.

Ibbotson was still asleep when I knocked on the glazed door, and the moment he caught sight of me he jumped out of bed and dashing to the door flung it open, embraced me, and next minute was dancing round the leopard which the men had deposited on the verandah. Shouting for tea, and a hot bath for me, he called for his stenographer and dictated telegrams to the Government, the press, and my sister, and a cable to Jean. Not one question had he asked, for he knew that the leopard which I had brought home at that early hour was the man-eater, so what need was there for questions? On that previous occasion—in spite of all the evidence that had been produced—I had maintained that the leopard killed in the gin-trap was not the man-eater, and on this occasion I had said nothing.

Ibbotson had carried a heavy responsibility since October of the previous year, for to him was left the answering of questions of Councillors anxious to please their constituents, of Government officials who were daily getting more alarmed at the mounting death-toll, and of a press that was clamouring for results. His position had for a long time been like that of the head of a police force who, knowing the identity of a noted criminal, was unable to prevent his committing further crimes, and for this was being badgered on all sides. Little wonder then that Ibbotson on that 2nd of May 1926 was the happiest man I had even seen, for not only was he now able to inform all concerned that the criminal had been executed, but he was also able to tell the people from the bazaars, and from the surrounding villages, and the pilgrims, all of whom were swarming into the compound of the Inspection Bungalow, that the evil spirit that had tormented them for eight long years was now dead.

After emptying a pot of tea and having a hot bath I tried to get a little sleep, but fear of a repetition of the cramps that twisted my feet, and from which I was only relieved by the vigorous ministrations of Ibbotson, brought me out of bed. Then Ibbotson and I measured the leopard, and carefully examined it. The following are the results of our measurements and of our examination.

MEASUREMENTS

Length, between pegs	7 feet, 6 inches
Length, over curves	7 feet, 10 inches

[Note: these measurements were taken after the leopard had been dead twelve hours.]

DESCRIPTION

Colour:	Light straw.
Hair:	Short and brittle.
Whiskers:	None.
Teeth:	Worn and discoloured, one canine tooth broken.
Tongue and mouth:	Black.
Wounds:	One fresh bullet-wound in right shoulder.
	One old bullet-wound in pad of left hind foot, and part of one toe and one claw missing from same foot.
	Several deep and partly-healed cuts on head.
	One deep and partly-healed cut on right hind leg.
	Several partly-healed cuts on tail.
	One partly-healed wound on stifle of left hind leg.

I am unable to account for the leopard's tongue and mouth being black. It was suggested that this might have been caused by cyanide, but whether this was so or not I cannot say. Of the partly-healed wounds, those on the head, right hind leg, and tail were acquired in his fight at Bhainswara, and the one on the stifle of his left hind leg was the result of his having been caught in the gin-trap, for the piece of skin and tuft of hair we found in the trap fitted into this wound. The injuries on the left hind foot were the result of the bullet fired on the bridge by the young army officer in 1921. When skinning the leopard later, I found a pellet of buckshot embedded in the skin of his chest which an Indian Christian—years later—claimed he had fired at the leopard the year it became a man-eater.

After Ibbotson and I had measured and examined the leopard it was laid in the shade of a tree, and throughout the day thousands of men, women, and children came to see it.

When the people of our hills visit an individual for any particular purpose, as for instance to show their gratitude or to express their thanks, it is customary for them not to go on their mission empty-handed. A rose, a marigold, or a few petals of either flower, suffices, and the gift is proffered in hands cupped together. When the recipient has touched the gift with the tips of the fingers of his right hand, the person proffering the gift goes through the motion of pouring the gift on to the recipient's feet, in the same manner as if his cupped hands contained water.

I have on other occasions witnessed gratitude, but never as I witnessed it that day at Rudraprayag, first at the Inspection Bungalow and later at a reception in the bazaar.

'He killed our only son, *sahib*, and we being old, our house is now desolate.'

'He ate the mother of my five children, and the youngest is but a few months old, and there is none in the home now to care for the children, or to cook the food.'

'My son was taken ill at night and no one dared go to the hospital for medicine, and so he died.'

Tragedy upon pitiful tragedy, and while I listened, the ground around my feet was strewn with flowers.

EPILOGUE

The events I have narrated took place between 1925 and 1926. Sixteen years later, in 1942, I was doing a war job in Meerut and my sister and I were invited one day by Colonel Flye to help entertain wounded men at a garden party. The men, some fifty or sixty in number, and from all parts of India, were sitting round a tennis-court just finishing a sumptuous tea, and getting to the smoking stage, when we arrived. Taking opposite sides of the court, my sister and I started to go round the circle.

The men were all from the Middle East, and, after a rest, were to be sent to their homes, some on leave, and some on discharge. Music, in the form of a gramophone with Indian records, had been provided by Mrs Flye, and as my sister and I had been requested to stay until the party gave over—which would be in about two hours' time—we had ample time to make our circuit of the wounded men.

I had got about halfway round the circle when I came to a boy sitting in a low chair; he had been grievously wounded, and on the ground near his chair were two crutches. At my approach he very painfully slid off his chair and attempted to put his head on my feet. He was woefully light, for he had spent many months in hospital, and when I had picked him up and made him comfortable in his chair, he said; 'I have been talking with your lady sister, and when I told her I was a Garhwali, she told me who you were. I was a small boy when you shot the man-eater, and as our village is far from Rudraprayag I was not able to walk there, and my father not being strong was unable to carry me, so I had to stay at home. When my father returned he told me he had seen the man-eater, and that with his own eyes he had seen the *sahib* who had shot it. He also told me of the sweets that had been distributed that day—his share of which he had brought back for me—and of the great crowds he had seen. And now, *sahib*, I will go back to my home with great joy in my heart, for I shall be able to tell my father that with my own eyes I have seen you and, maybe, if I can get anyone to carry me to the fair that is held every year at Rudraprayag to commemorate the death of the man-eater, I shall tell all the people I meet there that I have seen and had speech with you.'

A cripple, on the threshold of manhood, returning from the wars with a broken body, with no thought of telling of brave deeds done, but only eager to tell his father that with his own eyes he had seen the man who years ago he had not had the opportunity of seeing, a man whose only claim to remembrance was that he had fired one accurate shot.

A typical son of Garhwal, of that simple and hardy hill-folk; and of that greater India, whose sons only those few who live among them are privileged to know. It is these big-hearted sons of the soil, no matter what their caste or creed, who will one day weld the contending factions into a composite whole, and make of India a great nation.